ASSIMILATING IN AMERICA

Prophetic Perspectives on 50 Years of Integration

Kenneth W. Burrough

Dedication

To My Lord & Savior Jesus Christ
Thank You LORD, I live to serve You.

This book is Dedicated
To the 5 children You've blessed me with.

Rest in Peace
Mattie Ann Callier-Spears

Forward

Assimilating in America was self-published nearly 20 years ago while I was living in Portland, Oregon.

It started out as a series of notes that I had gleaned over the years from a few hundred books I had studied, and developed into an eight chapter book before I knew it.

Given all that has transpired since that time, one would suspect that perhaps the perspectives and conclusions originally inspired might have changed.

However, the reverse is not only the case, but it's truths have become even more evident and eye-opening. This is one of the primary characteristics of an authentic prophetic perspective.

This new, updated version remains about 90% true to the original in content, however, there has been absolutely no compromising of the themes that developed back then. Points have simply been clarified, and redundancy reduced.

Acknowledgments

I wish to acknowledge the following people for their inspiration and influence:

Rev. Olester M. Burrough Sr. & Mrs. Loetta Burrough
Best Mom and Dad in the world! – *Thank you for raising us in the church.*

Dr. Martin Luther King Jr.
Gifted minister, civil rights leader, social reformer, author and 1964 Nobel Peace Prize winner. – *Thank you for Strength to Love.*

Dr. James H. Cone
Brilliant theologian, minister and author – *Thank you for Black Theology.*

Dr. Cheik Anta Diop
Exceptional African Egyptologist, historian, linguist, anthropologist and author – *Thank you for helping me love my native land.*

Table Of Contents

Preface

Anyone who's committed to taking a prophetic perspective will inevitably end up offending some very decent people. This is a very unfortunate consequence, especially if you've come to know a few personally.

Nevertheless, even decent people often embrace and perpetuate ideas that *someone* is obligated to confront.

Several significant historic atrocities attest to this. However three in particular should supply more than adequate evidence.

> The Holocaust
> Slavery
> Apartheid

Notwithstanding the tremendous humanitarian responses generated eventually by a significant number of decent people long after these atrocities had become systematic and customary, less attention has been paid to the involvement of decent people before and during their occurrences.

But the heart wrenching truth is that they held quite tightly to their ideals of decency and morality as they witnessed their fellow human beings being sold, hanged, gassed, whipped, burned, emasculated, enslaved, dehumanized and discriminated against, didn't they?

They even expected the victims of these heartless and inhuman abominations to be patient and understanding while it was all being worked out, didn't they?

And to add insult to injury, decent people even allowed these barbaric events to occur after being confronted by the exceptional likes of Dietrich Bonhoeffer in Germany, the Abolitionists in America and Bishop Tutu in South Africa.

Yet they still chose to co-sign the cultural rhetoric and help perpetuate the atrocities, didn't they?

Why?

Why didn't any significant number of decent people recognize any of these obvious evils and confront them?

Were they all that ignorant?? Were they all so afraid of the evil that they feared for their very own lives?

Or were they all just deceived?

For all we know they might have even sensed the evil themselves and still elected to tolerate or embrace it in secret.

Whatever their reasons were, Martin Niemoller [1] solemnly reflects upon the fruits of decent people in his infamous poem, "First They Came". The version inscribed at the New England Holocaust Memorial in Boston reads as follows:

> They came first for the Communists,
> and I didn't speak up because I wasn't a Communist.
>
> Then they came for the Jews,
> and I didn't speak up because I wasn't a Jew.
>
> Then they came for the trade unionists,
> and I didn't speak up because I wasn't a trade unionist.
>
> Then they came for the Catholics,
> and I didn't speak up because I was a Protestant.
>
> Then they came for me,
> and by that time no one was left to speak up.

While it's bad enough that most of the decent people in these three different scenarios chose to either co-sign or tolerate these atrocities, what's worse is that their unethical ideas and behaviors could easily be explained by the teachings of their moral leaders.

According to the MSN Encarta Encyclopedia website:

> Despite their opposition to Hitler's racial doctrine, Catholic and other Christian church leaders failed to take a public stand against his anti-Semitic policies.

> The major Christian churches [...] failed to react when the Nazis introduced racial legislation, instigated physical attacks on Jews, or began the deportation and extermination of Jews.

> The pope never criticized the persecution of the Jews in an encyclical, nor did he ever threaten to excommunicate Hitler, nominally a Catholic, or other Catholics involved in the Holocaust.

> Moreover, although the pope and his advisers were fully informed about the extermination of the Jews during World War II, they refused to condemn it...

And according to the African Christianity website:

> Afrikaners (White people in South Africa) see themselves as the obedient people of God shaping a society according to Biblical, Christian principles. The Afrikaners saw strong parallels between themselves as the people of God, and the Biblical nation of Israel as the people of God.

> For historical reasons the Afrikaner community has felt itself to be an embattled minority struggling to be obedient to God while faced with hostile forces all around trying to prevent it from doing so.

This sense of threat – from the black majority and from the powerful English supported by liberal world opinion, has led the Afrikaner churches to develop racist and exclusivistic responses, and to defend those responses theologically.

Then finally, according to Thomas Paine, founding member of America's first anti-slavery society:

"That some desperate wretches should be willing to steal and enslave men by violence and murder for gain is rather lamentable than strange.

But that many civilized, nay, Christianized people should approve, and be concerned in the savage practice, is surprising; and still persist, though it has been so often proved contrary to the light of nature, to every principle of Justice and Humanity ...

Most shocking of all is alleging the sacred scriptures to favour this wicked practice."

In light of the fact that the "Christians" in America also, forced us to establish our own places of worship, perpetuated the arrogant misconception of a White Jesus, and sustained the malicious misinterpretation of a curse on black skin, I've *never* wondered why so many of us Black people reject Christianity in favor of other standards.

Nor have I ever wondered why so many decent White Americans persist in embracing such a whitewashed facsimile of this "land healing" faith.

Considering the inconsistent history and expression of the Christian faith here in America, let alone on the earth itself, it should amaze just about anyone in their right mind why so many of us continue to embrace it so wholeheartedly.

I encourage you to continue reading and discover why.

Joy 'n Pain

Comedian Jonathan Slocumb once joked that if Dr. Martin Luther King Jr. were alive today he'd most likely be delivering a very different kind of speech. A speech that might more appropriately be entitled, "I Never Dreamed." *(Slocumb)*

He proceeded by elaborating on some of the funnier aspects of our integration here in America that Dr. King almost certainly never would have dreamed of seeing decades later.

Like so many of the profound insights I've heard expressed by Black comedians over the years, this one here had not only tickled me, but it also cut me like a knife.

This was quite a bittersweet reality he had hit upon. After all, we had indeed inherited Dr. King's Dream. Yet, we had also inherited Malcolm's Nightmare.

Certainly, integration had been funny at some points. (Black people seem to find something funny in almost everything, even tragedy). However, above all, it had been an immeasurable assortment of joys and pains.

Consequently, the *agonies and ecstasies* engendered as a result of having to cautiously navigate this conflicted existence here in America have been either the principal or incidental focus of nearly all of our personalities and institutions ever since.

Whereas those *inconsistencies* and *contradictions* that have emerged among us as a consequence of being compelled to assume a foreign identity, history, and culture here, have never received quite as much consideration.

Nor have the *oddities and absurdities* that have surfaced among Americans as repercussions to oppressing and slaughtering people while claiming "Christian" ideals been adequately scrutinized.

Accordingly, this country is currently experiencing nothing less than the negative effects of such culture and identity altering Americanisms as:

> Slave Laws (or Codes)
> Slave Religion
> White Religion
> White History
> Western Science
> American Media

Having neglected to adequately consider the full extent to which all this obviously influential programming has negatively affected us, has of course had nothing but adverse effects.

Perhaps one of the worst is that it's led us to believe that everything American is superior, and everything African is "inferior".

And it's no wonder, America's experts wrote big thick books using big long words that they learned in the same institutions that we worship today, to prove it.

Furthermore, they used the same science and theology that we worship today to say that we were not even worthy of human dignity because of our skin color, our brain size, and even a curse from God Himself.

And now a whole new generation of America's social scientists are arrogantly advancing yet another half-baked theory regarding our responses to experiences they couldn't begin to bear.

Their assumption goes like this: Racism, discrimination and poverty are no longer the main instigators of African-American shortcomings and shame in this country. They must therefore be the consequence of some sort of inherited cultural deficiency.

Speculations such as this have only helped widen the divide between us and sustain the true tragedy of our lifetime, which is the persistent alienation existing between the affluent inheritors of our forefathers' forced free labor, and us, their disinherited and assimilating descendants.

But here's the real kicker. Because we've become so pathetically unaware of our own native, pre-colonial, African identity, ethics, and culture, we're in no position to argue the point!

We're in no position to inform anyone that we were actually a whole lot safer living with our lions, tigers and bears than we are with America's crack, alcohol, guns and racists.

We're in no position to enlighten anyone either that we were much more content working with nature and the Creator than we are with this heartless, forgive-less and anti-social hardware.

Nor do we know enough to tell anyone that we were way more safe and virtuous living half-naked at home than we are living fully clothed in their sexually perverted society.

But, more than anything else, we're in no position to inform them that the *real God* was already in Africa before the White man brought his there!

Having neglected to adequately consider the full extent to which America's negative programming has affected us has not only prompted us to forget about home, *but to hate home.*

Our vast and glorious homeland and all of her diverse inhabitants and cultures have become dark, dangerous and undesirable to us, hasn't it?

We no longer remember nor do we hunger for our homeland's exceptional beauty or abundant resources anymore, do we?

Neither do we recall any of our native values and virtues.

And now it no longer matters that the whole world wants to possess and control the Motherland or that the tourism industry wants to exploit her.

All we're able to do is mimic, exaggerate and validate each and every negative thing this country's teachers, preachers and media taught us about our savage and embarrassing Dark Continent.

However, truth be told, a lot of Africans these days have every right to perceive us as the savage and embarrassing ones, don't they?

We're the ones who are illegitimate citizens of a country that has consistently disrespected us. We never signed any documents, swore any oaths, or went to any classes to become Americans, did we?

And we weren't given the right hand of fellowship either, were we?

Our Christian churches are still embarrassments to this country's Christian reputation over 50 years following integration, aren't they?

And African-Americans are yet and still the visible and audible reminders of this country's past and present inhumanities and contradictions. We are still anomalies and amendments in her constitutions and declarations.

Yet and still, we remain in hot pursuit of her dreams and treasures, don't we?

By any means necessary.

If indeed Dr. King were alive today in this age of absurdities, he'd very likely be declaring (spoken in Dr. King's voice):

> "I never dreamed that the American Negro's long overdue and anxiously awaited integration here in this great Promised Land of opportunity and ample resources, would ever come to engender such a shameless, Godless, and greedy generation of young, gifted and Black entrepreneurs!"

> "Who having become so pathetically desperate to lay hold to a golden promise so long deferred have quickly and eagerly sold away the dignity, sanctity and character of their own mothers, sisters and daughters."

> "I never dreamed!!"

So before any Black person in this country gets the nerve to criticize Africa or it's way of life, they need to seriously consider all of the inconsistencies and absurdities they are living with first.

Especially before they think about defending and dying for this so-called "freedom".

This is nothing more than freedom to do evil! This is freedom to worship idols, abuse weapons, market pornography and hop from bed to bed!

And this is freedom to abuse and exploit God's gift of Choice too. This is NOT civilized or advanced!

This freedom exploits our lower nature. It is Neanderthalic, regressive, and an outright perversion of real freedom!

For far too many of us African-Americans, America's inconsistencies and contradictions have been far too consistent for far too long.

And having to cautiously negotiate them all individually and instinctively has been more than overwhelming to say the least.

Consequently, many of us have tuned them out and consumed

ourselves instead with some of this country's more palatable social pacifiers like the Playoffs, or some Awards show, or the pursuit of some ultimate sexual experience.

However, the consequences of such life deferred has been nothing less than a society of oppressed minorities who've come to consider themselves citizens of a country that has consistently perpetuated insults and brutalities against them.

The fact that some of us occasionally receive some praise and success certainly seems to placate many of us. But for the rest, the inconsistencies have engendered some sort of a love-hate relationship with this country that's coming across as dysfunction.

The rest of the world has to be whispering, "boy, they sure seem to complain a lot about a country they claim to love so much!"

I'm convinced modern mental health professionals would strongly suggest any individual willingly remaining in a relationship that is beset with habitually inconsistent acts of admiration and disrespect would be considered behaving insensibly.

Neither would they be considered behaving sensibly if they persisted in harboring false impressions about the perpetrators of these inconsistent acts.

In reality, we've become a lot like the people in Scripture who have eyes but can't see, and ears but can't hear.

And just like them, its because we've gotten distracted by the same idols, like money, power and sex and the people who symbolize them, rather than survival or empowerment.

It's helped numb us to some realities that most experts consider traumatic. Like having our children grow up in communities full of hustlers, gang members and drug pushers.

And it's helped buffer us from all the fatherlessness, homelessness and hopelessness that festers throughout our neighborhoods.

We don't want a "finger put in our ear, or spit on our eyes" because we don't want to know that the bittersweet reality of life has caused us to tolerate far too many great dilemmas.

Nor do we want to know how high the costs associated with living a life of contradictions are, either.

Not unless you make it sound funny and frivolous, like Chris Rock:

> "If you're black, America's like the uncle that paid your way through college — but molested you."

However, the truth be told, America is more like the uncle who hates Michael Jackson, Bill Cosby and OJ, but introduced you to pornography, perversion and violence.

She's like that relative who begs you for money to feed starving children around the world, but constantly wastes an ungodly amount of the vital resource for the sake of a profit or a laugh.

No wonder the country's institutions are falling apart left and right. The Boy Scouts. Churches. Families. Law Enforcement. Etc.

Once I started critically considering all of this country's inconsistencies, absurdities and contradictions, I couldn't help but come to two conclusions:

Number One: America's "Christians" are nothing more than perpetrators, and Number Two: America never was truly a Christian nation.

Otherwise adultery, fornication and sodomy would still be illegal. And the people committing them would not be referred to in positive terms, like "players", "playboys" or "gay".

Otherwise it's citizens wouldn't be allowed to form "civil unions" and have them re-defined as "marriages". Nor would bestiality be legal in about 10 of her states and complicated in several others.

Before long it'll be okay to be "on the down low" in this country, or to marry an animal!

But what else should we expect from a culture that was founded upon treating it's mothers, sisters, and daughters like second class citizens while they exploited them all at the same time?

No wonder American women are exploiting themselves now. So the nation compensates by legalizing the murder of its unborn babies.

How can anyone expect a society that's callous enough to rationalize and legalize the murder of its innocent, unborn babies to have a problem legitimizing the holocaust of its minorities?

America.

Fornicate responsibly, kill babies responsibly, gamble responsibly, get drunk responsibly, get violent responsibly, waste food responsibly!

Please!

Buying into a way of life like this can only conclude in people living inconsistent and unfulfilled lives that make little to no sense ... suicidal.

The fact that inconsistencies such as these are so easily accepted by most Americans today clearly accounts for how they can claim to love the God of the Bible, and simultaneously displace the timeless truths of His Book with their own modern scientific theories.

It also accounts for how they can claim to love the precious living earth He created for us all to cultivate, protect and enjoy, while simultaneously promoting an economic ethic that allows and encourages greedy people to rape and pollute it.

However Americans are far too advanced to be confused, so it has to be nothing less than their superior *intellect* that allows them to do so.

Sarcasm aside, it's far more likely the fact that they are much less affected by their country's inconsistencies and atrocities that allows them to reconcile such things.

But so much for them. What about us?

As a Black man with a pretty healthy dose of dignity, I'd feel fairly foolish bragging on a nation that describes blackness as something negative and evil in at least 60 different ways, while describing whiteness as something favorable in twice as many.

No wonder we've been the perpetual victims of inferior incomes, piss-poor housing, discriminatory financing and inadequate health care here.

Once you factor in the personal bigotry we put up with daily, you're no longer surprised we've got the shortest life expectancy rates.

It seems to me this country loves our music, loves our mannerisms, loves our athletic ability, loves our fashion innovation, and loves our lingo, *but hates us.*

How long is it gonna take us to see that there's something's really wrong with a country that consumes, produces, promotes, and admires so much violence, immorality, greed and crime, yet simultaneously claims to be a Christian nation?

Even though the natives were insightful enough to see all of this inconsistent, duality in American culture (which they referred to as a "forked-tongue"), they didn't respond to it properly, unfortunately.

So how long will we be blinded by foreign ideals?

How long will we senselessly waste our allegiance on a country whose alleged peacekeepers have become so brutal and deluded that they habitually harass and persecute people who look like us?

How long before we stop cuddling up to a country whose justice system is unfairly punishing us with disproportionate jail sentences for being nothing more than victims of race based job discrimination?

And how long before we stop counting on a country whose educational system is actually the primary source of our mis-education?

In spite of the fact that the American educational system accomplishes some good and necessary things for its citizen's, at the same time it misleads them morally. [2]

It misleads them with its false histories, tainted ideologies, and it's "greater than God" science.

It encourages mainstream Americans to believe in and then broadcast inferiority theories, evolution theories, economic theories, and historic perceptions as if they were absolute truth!

How arrogant!

For those who would point to all the progress we've made since we've been here as evidence of the country's integrity, first of all I'd say we fought tooth and nail for every bit of it. Nobody gave us anything.

And then I'd suggest we measure the progress we've made by the wisdom of Malcolm, whose unforgettable quote has apparently gone forgotten.

> "If you stick a knife in my back nine inches and pull it out six inches, there's no progress. If you pull it all the way out that's not progress. Progress is healing the wound that the blow made."

Personally, I thank God for the three-inch withdrawal, and I'm very grateful for the Black and White martyrs who sacrificed for it. Because of them, I'm personally living in that joy and progress, for the most part.

However, in spite of how good things might be for me personally, it'll never be acceptable that any part of the knife remains in our collective back.

Why?

Because I still identify with every unarmed and innocent Black man, woman and child who has a cop's knife stuck in their back.

While the insecure, resentful and hypocrites who prey on them like cannibals, yet tremble at our real thugs, have the audacity to tell everyone that violence is not the way.

And because I still identify with every struggling Black business, professional and worker out there who has a company's knife stuck in their back.

These rackets are real drunk on marketing and branding, but allergic to diversity and inclusion.

And when you get right down to it, they are really nothing more than experts at sustaining this country's ungodly wealth gap.

Their C-suites and numbers don't lie like their commercials.

Integration

As mentioned earlier, the more common perception concerning the persistent pains of Black people here in America is that they are more attributable to various deep-seated defects within our ethics or value system.

This line of reasoning asserts that if we were just more inclined to parenting and saving rather than partying and complaining, we just might become as successful as mainstream Americans.

The primary fault of this thought process however is that it neglects to consider one important detail.

Stereotypical shortcomings such as these did not start to characterize Black people until we were forced to integrate into this social and cultural environment.

Prior to our integration into American society, our African ethic was characterized by its humility, hospitality, generosity, patience, tolerance, practicality, discernment, justice, improvisation, forgiveness and spirituality *(Paris)*.

Black people possessed a particularly strong family structure and we embraced a financial ethic now known as cooperative economics.

Our legacy included plenty of successful and enduring civilizations that are still amazing the world today, and the continuity of these ethics and values from Africa to America has been clearly established by Peter J. Paris, Professor Emeritus of Christian Social Ethics at Princeton Theological Seminary.

"From extensive comparative research and personal travel, Paris shows how such values were retained and modified in the diaspora, most notably in African-American religious and moral thought and its practice.

Traditional understandings of God, ancestral spirits, tribal community, family belonging, reciprocity, personal destiny, and agency have not only survived great cultural upheavals but remarkably even been enriched and enlivened."

It is only after our large-scale integration into American society, which was won by the Civil Rights generation, that we begin to experience a serious wholesale compromise of these traditional African values and ethics.

Let me say that again.

It is only after our large-scale integration into American society, which was won by the Civil Rights generation, that we begin to experience a serious wholesale compromise of our traditional African values and ethics.[3]

Anyone gullible enough to assume that a 10% poor and oppressed minority integrating into the most powerful country in the world possessed enough influence to initiate a wholesale compromise of its values has been seriously deceived.

They have been deluded into believing that we possessed enough power and influence to instigate America's:

Sexual Liberation Movement

Generation Gap

Secular Humanism Era

Drug Abuse Epidemic

Abortion Rights Movement

Divorce Epidemic

Feminist Movement

They have been hoodwinked, as Malcolm would say. Black people in America had nothing to do with any of her institutional breakdowns.

We didn't cause this country's families to fall apart left and right, or its colleges to become centers of social protest, nor its corporations to become icons of irresponsibility and greed.

And in spite of the fact that we did initiate our share of riots, rebellions and protests, they were only our instinctive responses to America's persistent injustices.

They were never designed to be subversive. Nor were they ever intended to corrupt American society. Actually quite the contrary!

The attitudes and the environment that produced America's cultural upheavals had been set into motion long before we ever got here.

We merely plunged into this cultural "river, which was already rushing to the new frontier".

And although most of these major social movements were in response to government and institutional oppression, local and national governments became even more oppressive and violent in response to them.

Young White college students and hippies alike knew this, and their response to it all was a counter-culture movement that continues to this day, exposing and opposing their country's corruption and hypocrisy.

The Temptations put it this way years ago:

> People moving out, people moving in
> Why, because of the color of their skin.
> Run, run, run but you sure can't hide.
> An eye for an eye, a tooth for a tooth

Vote for me and I'll set you free.
Rap on, brother, rap on.
Well, the only person talking about love thy brother
is the preacher.
And it seems nobody's interested in learning but the teacher.
Segregation, determination, demonstration, integration.
Aggravation, humiliation, obligation to our nation.
Ball of Confusion!
Oh yeah, that's what the world is today.
The sales of pills are at an all time high.
Young folks walking round with their heads in the sky.
The cities ablaze in the summer time
And oh, the beat goes on.
Evolution, revolution, gun control, sound of soul.
Shooting rockets to the moon, kids growing up too soon.
Politicians say more taxes will solve everything.
And the band played on.
So, round and around and around we go.
Where the world's headed, nobody knows.

Although I'm convinced that most of the corruptions in American society were more likely the fruits of their overwhelming and overflowing hypocrisies, arrogance and injustices, just like their Civil War, that's not the point.

The point is that most Black people here in America today integrated into a society and a culture that was in the process of being transformed by revolutionary social movements, and not into the one that *might have* existed before.

Not into the one that *might have* been characterized by its morality and its "Happy Days" family values, had it not been for the way so-called "Christian" Americans treated their neighbors, the Negroes.[4]

And now just over 50 years later, subsequent to integration, hindsight reveals that we have inherited more than just Dr. King's

Dream. And we've inherited more than just Malcolm's Nightmare as well.

We have inherited the American's Fantasy. This fantasy is nothing less than the romantic conviction that this country is in some way destined by God to bless the whole world.

It's also known as a superiority complex and nearly every individual in America gets infected with this pretense in their elementary institutions by whoever teaches them Manifest Destiny.

Embracing this foreign fantasy has generated a major fracture in our traditional African cultural values and stroked some other intrinsic human qualities within us, causing them to grow.

Consequently, many of us have become much more arrogant, aggressive, greedy, individualistic, selfish, spoiled, secular, superficial, impatient, intolerant, and hostile. The exact opposite of what we were in Africa.

I've come to believe that part of the reason Americans believe our native culture is to blame for our present problems is related to another significant shortcoming in Western culture.

This particular failing is one that's influenced many of its decent, intelligent and reasonable citizens to miss a lot of what's obvious to the rest of the world.

The Bible characterizes it as "straining a gnat and swallowing a camel".

It was also alluded to in an intuitive poem composed by Terry Kettering entitled, "The Elephant in the Room" and in a book written by South African theologian Allan Aubrey Boesak, entitled, "Farewell to Innocence."

It appears to be the programmed response that smart people make to reconcile their savage inclinations.

These people can appreciate and celebrate the miracle of birth and life and still market immorality and abortion.

They can filter and sift through statistics of world poverty and hunger and still throw away food like it was yesterday's garbage.

They can stretch and strain the significance of freedom and justice and still steal and abuse millions of people who weren't even bothering them.

And while it's bad enough that countless numbers of secular American individuals and institutions have guiltlessly accepted and perpetuated such shortcomings for several hundred years now, what's worse is that their churches have been just as complicit.

Their reputations for obsessing over the insignificant things like mega buildings and mega gatherings while failing to regard the elephants of segregated and loveless churches is now unparalleled.

And just like the pharisees, they travel over land and sea to win a single convert, but when they have succeeded, they make them twice as much a child of hell as they are, while communities in America are drowning in poverty.

Everything they do is for attention. Their lives are as large as the celebrities. But none of them are known for their justice, mercy and faithfulness.

Once my eyes and ears were opened to all this, I began to understand that it was absolutely impossible for all of this madness *not* to affect us.

The natural consequences of integration was not only a merging and sharing of the obvious qualities and practices between groups, like sex and intellect, but the less obvious also, like morals and ideals.

Understanding who contributed what was simply a matter of making a legitimate investigation into each group's culture before they began to merge.

The results of my own personal look into each before they merged, gradually began to conflict radically with nearly everything I had learned in the American educational system.

But it also began to clear up many of the contradictions, quandaries, and paradoxes I had contemplated over the years.

I began to see that we Black people here in America were not actually predisposed or inclined to compromising our morals and victimizing each other, but that we were simply assimilating some of the more negative aspects of American culture.

I also began to understand just how that angry and militant Black rapper, Ice Cube, could mutate right before my very eyes into a rich, happy and funny actor.

And I finally began to understand just why it was that the prosperous Black people in America did not unite.

It was only after I had begun to consider the possibility that our original African value system had been compromised once it came into contact with American culture that I began to understand these irregularities.

Let me say that again ...

It was only after I had begun to consider the possibility that our original African value system had been compromised once it came into contact with American culture that I began to understand these irregularities.

Now of course if you asked almost any American, of almost any color sadly, they would be shocked by such an allegation.

They would suggest we should still be thanking our God that our ancestors were lucky enough to get caught and dragged from the huts, heathenism and barbarism of Africa to this wonderful new world in order to share in American glory.

Additionally, they would claim that in reality, American culture was compromised as a result of coming into contact with our way of life.

Well, this is because most Americans are still relying upon research based upon outdated, racist resources.

That's why Jesus Christ, the first-century Jew is still White in most current American Christian literature and media, in spite of the obvious historical and Biblical inaccuracy (*Dillard 182-185*).

That's also why most Americans are still proud to embrace their violent, aggressive and devious beginnings.

It would be impossible to keep them proud if this outdated, racist research were not predominating in their society.

God forbid their children ever being taught the likes of Howard Zinn's, "A People's History of the United States" in their elementary classrooms.

It's just as unlikely as *us* ever becoming aware of the research Black scholars have performed on our own native ethics and values.

Oppression

One of the worst consequences yet of our integration here in America has been this very vicious cycle of poverty in which we presently find ourselves.

And since all cycles have elusive sources and solutions, they usually keep everyone pointing fingers at each other instead of evaluating their own part in the mess.

They generate fruitless "chicken or egg first" discussions that have already left so many in a perpetual state of analysis paralysis.

Here in America this inhuman cycle has clearly combined with the insatiable system of capitalism to create one hell of a social catastrophe.

And while that's bad enough, what's worse is that this catastrophe has generated such a substantial economy that it's now absolutely essential for the millions of mainstream families who've come to depend upon its revenues, to live their comfortable lives.

However, those of us who find ourselves trapped in the cycle become subjected to a web of extra obstacles, challenges, requirements, and nonsense that this shadow economy requires to survive.

If we happen to work our way out of the web, we are usually considered exceptional. We're typically rather arrogant much like our exemplars, and are happily used as symbols of success.

If we happen to express any compassion at all, it's usually followed up by the contemptuous phrase, "But you should've known better!" We buy into the American dream because we just so happened to avoid the American nightmare.

Those of us who struggle with the web of extras are considered normal. But those of us who don't break free are blamed for being victims.

Once I began to see this dynamic from a prophetic perspective, I was absolutely blown away.

I had no idea that this country had used and was using tactics that had been condemned by the Bible's Prophets, not only to create, but to maintain the web.

> (Rich) people hide in secret places and wait to catch people. They hide, looking for people to hurt.
>
> They kill innocent people. Those bad people are like lions trying to catch the animals they will eat.
>
> They attack poor people. The poor people are caught in the traps [5] that the evil people make.
>
> Again and again, those bad people hurt poor, hurting people.
>
> *Psalms 10:8-10 (ERV).*
>
> There are evil men among my people. Those evil men are like men that make nets for catching birds.
>
> These men set their traps, but they catch men instead of birds.
>
> The houses of these evil men are full of lies, like a cage full of birds.
>
> Their lies made them rich and powerful. They have grown big and fat {from the evil things they have done}.

> There is no end to the evil things they do. They will not plead the case of children that have no parents.
>
> They will not help those orphans. They will not let poor people be judged fairly.
>
> *Jeremiah 5:26-28 (ERV).*

> You have made the people like fish in the sea. They are like little sea-animals without a leader.
>
> The enemy catches all of them with hooks and nets. The enemy catches them in his net and drags them in.
>
> And the enemy is very happy with what he caught. His net helps him live like a rich man and enjoy the best food.
>
> So the enemy worships his net. He makes sacrifices and burns incense to honor his net.
>
> Will he continue to take riches with his net? Will he continue destroying people without showing mercy?
>
> *Habakkuk 1:14-17 (ERV)*

Well, it should be rather obvious by now how it is that America's enlightened and advanced ministers and theologians have gotten away with either minimizing, misunderstanding and overlooking verses like these for so long, shouldn't it?

Besides the fact that very few of them had the guts or the moral ground to induce any guilt, shame or accountability among their rich and powerful parishioners, verses like these challenged and discredited their traditional, slave interpretations.

From my perspective, verses like these also help to explain why so many of us are locked up in this county's proliferating prison system, not to mention her emotional and spiritual prisons.

And likewise they help explain many of the messes in Africa and the Caribbean.

The fact that they're not very popular verses in American theology, let alone the Black church, also helps to explain why so many of us aren't finding The Faith relevant anymore.

You don't need to say a prayer or possess a seminary degree to understand verses like these. They speak for themselves to people who are willing to listen. A revelation like this certainly resonates within those Black individuals who are in tune with their heritage.

Initially the traps that were set up for us were simply physical in nature, but over time they've become more complex and common.

The newer varieties are not only targeting our youth, but our minds and souls as well, and it's a full time job trying to recognize and respond to them all.

So I no longer wonder why we aren't more focused and united. Not with all these distractions. We didn't have near as many traps laid for us before our large-scale integration in America.

Just a few of the more significant ones that have contributed to our struggles and poverty here have included:

Slave Religion

Legal and Illegal Discrimination

Social and Institutional Discrimination

Ghettos and a Culture of Poverty

Corrupt Law Enforcement

Prejudiced Laws and Courts

Prison Industrial Complex

Science

Corrupt/Substandard Education

A Culture of Excess

Drugs and Alcohol

Personal and Structural Violence

Pornography

Illegitimate Sex

Abortion

False Religion and Corrupt Teachers

Of course there are several others as well, but I'm not attempting to be comprehensive, I'm only trying to make a point.

The point being that in spite of all the dysfunction these traps must produce, it is still assumed to be our fault for getting caught in them.

It is our fault for allowing them to influence us. It's our fault for not eliminating them and it is our fault for sustaining them.

Personally I've heard enough of this rhetoric.

The strategies that have been concocted to subdue us both emotionally and spiritually have been nothing less than overwhelming and dehumanizing, and other cultures have been crushed under the weight of it.

There's a legitimate reason why the phrases, "I Am Somebody" and "Keep Hope Alive" struck such a resonant chord in so much of Black America.

Make no mistake about it, it's not unusual for grown men and women to grow hopeless, indifferent and explosive after experiencing enough rejections, broken promises, disrespect and dashed hopes.

Too many of us have been put through enough madness in this country to make most anyone in their right mind "wanna holla".

Personally, I know all too well the pain and the damage that these traps cause Black fathers as much as they cause Black families. It's all equally valid and devastating, but for us, it's a pain that hides quietly and festers.

It either erupts violently upon the people we do love (maybe too much) or it kills us from the inside out, softly and slowly. Either way, the whole family suffers.

Gil Scott-Heron expresses the hurt and hopelessness of a man so movingly in his song, "Pieces of a Man".

> Jagged, Jigsaw pieces,
> Tossed about the room
> I saw my grandma sweepin'
> With her old straw broom
> But she didn't what she was doin'
> She could hardly understand
> That she was really sweepin' up
> Pieces of a man.

Langston Hughes expresses it as well in his poem, "Harlem", better known as, "A Dream Deferred".

> What happens to a dream deferred?
> Does it dry up
> like a raisin in the sun?
> Or fester like a sore—
> And then run?
> Does it stink like rotten meat?
> Or crust and sugar over—
> like a syrupy sweet?
> Maybe it just sags
> like a heavy load.
> Or does it explode?

You've got to be extremely subtle and crafty to convince a

"civilized" nation that the same people they spent hundreds of years dehumanizing, brainwashing, discriminating against and oppressing are not supposed to manifest any enduring damage.

And then at the same time have your psychologists agree that it's normal for human beings who have been forced to navigate and endure these types of traps from the cradle to the grave, to manifest:

> Desperation
>
> Misery
>
> Escapism
>
> Rebellion
>
> Nihilism
>
> Perversion
>
> Powerlessness
>
> Apathy

It not only helps relieve you of any guilt or responsibility, but it's also easier to preach from the pulpit that the same people who endured these barbaric atrocities are the sustainers of their own poverty.

That's why most everyone is so amazed by those few Black people in America who become "roses that grow from concrete." [6]

Let's admit it, the concrete that has been laid for us to grow up in here in America might have certainly produced a few roses, but by and large it is designed to produce far more weeds.

And what makes our particular poverty and oppression so much more paradoxical is that it occurs in the midst of so much:

> Greed
>
> Arrogance
>
> Excess

Waste

Opportunity

It never ceases to amaze me just how so many decent people in America today can actually be so arrogant as to assume and expect that the multitudes of our young Black children being born and raised under such polarizing conditions will somehow miraculously be transformed into successful and personally responsible men and women, husbands and wives, mothers and fathers, workers and role models.

What makes it so much more the worse though, is that while these young Black children are being sucked into poverty's powerfully vicious cycle and further crushed under its incredible weight, decent people today are kicking back in their warm and cozy homes and easy chairs and offering up armchair commentary on how "those people" need to pull themselves up by the bootstraps and stop all that craziness.

I dare any one of them to pry themselves away from the cable TV, the golf course or their precious brand new SUV and try some Black Like Me therapy.

Now that would be the ultimate American reality TV show … and I want the credit for it.

The Black folk who harbor such unrealistic expectations of their underprivileged relatives *should* feel tons of shame, guilt and embarrassment every time another White person gathers enough guts and compassion to admit that they couldn't possibly bear the weight of racism, poverty and oppression here in their very own country.

Those of us Black folk who just so happen to overcome all the challenges and pressures of poverty and oppression and achieve the almighty American Dream need to remember one thing.

We're actually being showcased as poster children for a selfish, individualistic, idolatrous and therefore, inferior ideal. We need to remember that all that "I am an island" and "I am the master of my own destiny" jazz isn't from our culture.

And that America's mainstream celebrations of a few arrogant Buppies are really nothing more than unsubstantial, symbolic panaceas for the multitudes of our underprivileged relatives.

We need to be reminded from time to time that we are just as susceptible to being brought down by some of the same negative pressures in this nation as our disadvantaged relatives.

And we are just as prone to being influenced, persuaded, provoked, manipulated, compelled and destroyed for some of the very same reasons.

Assimilation

Several Black theologians including Dr. King himself compared the bondage and liberation of Black people in America to the bondage and liberation of the Hebrews in Egypt.

This approach not only helped them validate the legitimacy of our movement, but it also helped maintain the proper direction and goal.

Those of us new millennium Negroes who wish to continue benefiting from this cultural distinction must continue to see and evaluate ourselves in the light of this legitimate history.

Never before has this been more critical than right now, because quite clearly at some point in the recent past we as a people began to contract an acute case of cultural amnesia.

And what we're currently experiencing in this American social context is by and large a consequence of having done so.

We might not want to admit it, but following our full scale integration here in America, a significant number of us started compromising a lot of our traditional, native values in order to either simply fit in or to achieve the almighty American Dream, didn't we?

We also started idolizing this country's cultural heroes and embracing their values too, didn't we?

Well the results have been horrendous to say the least, and perhaps the most embarrassing evidence of this has been the frying of our hair.

However the most damaging evidence has been the serious decline in our musical integrity.

We spit shit these days!

Other major manifestations have included a considerable rise in those rich, arrogant and independent Black people who forgot where they came from, a significant decline in our Black churches' influence and respect in their communities and the proliferation of shameless, self-hating youngsters who could care less about our reputation as a people.

I contend that all this is primarily the consequence of our blind, illegitimate entry into the social stage of human culture known as assimilation.

We rushed into assimilation like we rushed into Walmart on the day after Christmas.

But what's worse, is that we rushed in under the presumption that once we hit this so-called "promised land" of America, our cultural values, our families and our churches would remain intact.

After all, America the beautiful ... God shed His grace on thee!

Boy, were we in for a surprise!

We sure might have thought we were assimilating into a nation founded upon Biblical principles and values, however its leaders and citizens alike have always acted a lot more like Babylonians.

I feel like I need to say that again.

We sure might have thought that we were assimilating into a nation founded upon Biblical principles and values, however its leaders and citizens alike have always acted a lot more like Babylonians.

I'll elaborate upon this allegation a little more in the chapter entitled Allegiances. For now however, I'll submit my understanding of assimilation and then recall the Biblical parallel of this phenomenon.

Essentially, assimilation is a social process whereby a minority group integrates into a mainstream or a majority and ultimately adopts, alters and or drops certain cultural qualities to varying degrees.

These cultural qualities can consist of a fairly wide range of characteristics, including phenotypes (physical features), habits, ethics and perspectives.

Although there may be an initial exchange of certain characteristics among the groups, ultimately the mainstream or the majority most often assimilates the minority.

Consequently, failing to properly navigate this phase of life can be and has been extremely hazardous for minorities.

As far as the Biblical parallel is concerned, the assimilation of the Jews' occurred in Babylon several hundred years after their liberation from Egypt.

After wandering in the desert for 40 years, they finally conquered and possessed the Promised Land, just as God had promised.

And following their conquest, they enjoyed several hundred years of significant peace, prosperity and progress as they grew into the kingdom God promised them they'd be.

However, it wasn't very long before their prosperity led to arrogance, idolatry, selfishness, greed and injustice.

Since you'll never see a major motion picture focusing on this period in their history, you'll have to consult one of two resources to substantiate this, either the Scripture itself, or some "rabbinical resources".

I, of course recommend Scripture, especially in light of the fact that it alone submits a brutally honest portrayal of this favored nation's moral decline. And this is just one of the many manifestations of its exceptional integrity.

Rabbinical resources on the other hand tend to view this period much more favorably than the Bible.

My research reveals that this is due primarily to the prosperity and prestige they attained during this period more than anything else.

And seldom does prosperity and influence not lead to some form of apostasy, yet apostasy always leads to chastisement.

This time it led to a second captivity in Babylon.

Then, after enduring 70 more years of captivity, the Jews were once again liberated and given the option of returning to their own homeland or remaining in Babylon.

Guess what they did? Most of them chose to stay in Babylon and continue on assimilating, just like we did.

Therefore I assert it's not only legitimate and logical, but instructive as well for us to start collectively comparing our current assimilation into American culture, to the Jews' assimilation into Babylonian culture.

Those Jews who did not fall in love with Babylon consisted primarily of the poor folks, the patriots and the Prophets.

They were the ones who, in Psalm 137, "wept by the rivers of Babylon."

They were the ones who sang, "If I forget thee, O Jerusalem, let my right hand forget her cunning. If I do not remember thee, let my tongue cleave to the roof of my mouth".

When the opportunity to go back home presented itself, this

kind of Jew left.

In spite of all the desolation, poverty and hard labor that lie ahead, they returned to their own homeland and rejoined those compatriots who hadn't been deported and managed to survive the ensuing wars.

For those who stayed in Babylon however, assimilating into the culture had its benefits for sure. But at the same time, it had one pivotal drawback ... and that was the assimilation of the spiritual leaders.

As a result of their newly assimilated, cosmopolitan lifestyle, and the new knowledge they received from the Babylonian's and Greek's educational system, the spiritual leaders of the Jews began to use philosophy, science, mysticism, mathematics, etc. to reinterpret and re-explain God's Word.

Over the next several hundred years, their reinterpretations and re-explanations were documented, assembled, and referred to even more so than the legitimate Scriptures themselves.

Since they were referred to more frequently, they eventually became more authoritative.

Prior to being documented they were known as the Oral Tradition. Afterwards they came to be known collectively as the Talmud, [7] and its mystical counterpart as the Cabala.

Jesus called it "the tradition of the elders" or "the traditions of men":

> "For the Pharisees and all the Jews do not eat unless they wash their hands in a special way, holding the tradition of the elders."

> Then the Pharisees and scribes asked Him, "Why do Your disciples not walk according to the tradition of the elders, but eat bread with unwashed hands?"

> He answered and said to them, "Well did Isaiah prophesy of you hypocrites, as it is written: 'This people honors Me with their lips, But their heart is far from Me. And in vain they worship Me, Teaching as doctrines the commandments of men."

> "For laying aside the commandment of God, you hold the tradition of men – the washing of pitchers and cups, and many other such things you do."

> He said to them, "All too well you reject the commandment of God, that you may keep your tradition." "... making the word of God of no effect through your tradition which you have handed down. And many such things you do"

> *Mark 7:3, 5-9, 13(NKJV)*

However honest and innocent some of their intentions may have been in the beginning, the end result was that those most important concepts of God's Word like truth, justice, mercy and faithfulness were ultimately compromised.

That's why Jesus Christ was so upset with the spiritual leaders in His day. They had become even more hypocritical, assimilated and ineffective than they had been in Old Testament times.

> Jesus said to the crowds and to his disciples: "The Pharisees and the teachers of the Law are experts in the Law of Moses. So obey everything they teach you, but don't do as they do."

> "After all, they say one thing and do something else. They pile heavy burdens on people's shoulders and won"t lift a finger to help. Everything they do is just to show off in front of others."

> "They even make a big show of wearing Scripture verses on their foreheads and arms, and they wear big tassels for everyone to see."

"They love the best seats at banquets and the front seats in the meeting places. And when they are in the market, they like to have people greet them as their teachers."

"But none of you should be called a teacher. You have only one teacher, and all of you are like brothers and sisters. Don't call anyone on earth your father. All of you have the same Father in heaven. None of you should be called the leader. The Messiah is your only leader."

"Whoever is the greatest should be the servant of the others. If you put yourself above others, you will be put down. But if you humble yourself, you will be honored."

"You Pharisees and teachers of the Law of Moses are in for trouble! You're nothing but show-offs. You lock people out of the kingdom of heaven. You won't go in yourselves, and you keep others from going in."

"You Pharisees and teachers of the Law of Moses are in for trouble! You're nothing but show-offs. You travel over land and sea to win one follower. And when you have done so, you make that person twice as fit for hell as you are."

"You are in for trouble! You are supposed to lead others, but you are blind"

Matthew 23:1-16(CEV).

"You Pharisees and teachers are show-offs, and you're in for trouble! You give God a tenth of the spices from your garden, such as mint, dill, and cumin. Yet you neglect the more important matters of the Law, such as justice, mercy, and faithfulness."

"These are the important things you should have done, though you should not have left the others undone either."

"You blind leaders! You strain out a small fly but swallow a camel."

"You Pharisees and teachers are show-offs, and you're in for trouble! You wash the outside of your cups and dishes, while inside there is nothing but greed and selfishness."

"You blind Pharisee! First clean the inside of a cup, and then the outside will also be clean."

"You Pharisees and teachers are in for trouble! You're nothing but show-offs. You're like tombs that have been whitewashed. On the outside they are beautiful, but inside they are full of bones and filth."

"That's what you are like. Outside you look good, but inside you are evil and only pretend to be good."

"You Pharisees and teachers are nothing but show-offs, and you're in for trouble! You build monuments for the prophets and decorate the tombs of good people. And you claim that you would not have taken part with your ancestors in killing the prophets."

"But you prove that you really are the relatives of the ones who killed the prophets. So keep on doing everything they did. You are nothing but snakes and the children of snakes! How can you escape going to hell?"

"I will send prophets and wise people and experts in the Law of Moses to you. But you will kill them or nail them to a cross or beat them in your meeting places or chase them from town to town. That's why you will be held guilty for the murder of every good person."

Matthew 23:23-35 (CEV).

This isn't a one-time condemnation either. There are more than a few supporting passages.

Now there can be no doubt that this compromising of Biblical themes and standards has not only been fully inherited by the typical American "Christian" leader, but perhaps even further developed.

It would be very easy for us to substitute the frequent references to "Pharisees and teachers" with that of "preachers and seminary professors" in the verses quoted above.

We've already noted how the American perspective has caused many of them to dissect, analyze and departmentalize some key events in history and thereby lose sight of the big picture.

We also can't help but notice how many of them have very clearly defaulted on their obligation to teach and model legitimate Biblical humility before their sheepish congregations.

Not to mention how similar their role was in the character assassination of this generation's messenger of love and justice, Dr. King.

And haven't their world evangelism efforts typically gone hand in hand with their capitalist endeavors?

How many nations have been conquered and corrupted as a consequence of this country blending some Bible with some Bullets and some Bucks?

Although America's spiritual leaders haven't gone through the trouble of creating a whole new religious guide like the Jews (yet), they are creating so many different versions of the Bible based on their new "discoveries" and "disciplines" that it's starting to get scary.

The fruits of their theology can clearly be seen in their national headlines. Wasn't it Malcolm who once alleged that a particular tragedy in America's headline was nothing more than a "chicken coming home to roost"?

The implication was that certain tragedies in this nation were nothing more than their foundational evils coming back to haunt them.

Therefore, rather than continuing to mimic the loveless, divisive and inadequate theology of these mainstream Western seminarians and preachers, I submit that the legitimate Black spiritual leader who is truly determined to develop his congregation's vertical and horizontal obligations here in America start aggressively and routinely incorporating the theology of two much more fruitful and legitimate resources.

The first and foundational resource must of course be those divinely inspired Old Testament Prophets, who had at one time boldly confronted several very similar trends and issues among their own people.

Although each one of them were charged with nothing less than fearlessly and relentlessly condemning all of the idolatry, infidelity, iniquity, and oppression as well as the social, moral and political corruption they discovered among God's Chosen people in particular, they also condemned it wherever it was found. [8]

Consequently, many of their insights, messages, and warnings are still very relevant for contemporary societies.

First of all, there's the inspired writings of the Prophet **Hosea.**

Just by virtue of the fact that the first three chapters of his book candidly portrays and confronts two of America's more notorious social problems, which are infidelity and promiscuity, it appears to be tailor-made for those of us who've become victims of their appeal.

Then there is the divine revelation of the Prophet **Amos.** This book proved to be even more significant for me as a Black man in America.

I'm sure his objections to the twisted justice of his day are quite relevant to a lot of us. He described it as "a bitter pill for the poor and the oppressed."

"Righteousness and fair play are meaningless fictions to you," he wrote of his leaders. "How you hate honest judges! How you hate to tell the truth!

You trample the poor and steal what little they have through taxes and unfair rent. You oppress good people by taking bribes and deprive the poor of justice in the courts."

Then he admonishes them to remodel their courts into true halls of justice, and he informs them that the LORD wants to see "a mighty flood of justice" and "a river of righteous living that will never run dry."

I'm inclined to believe a lot of Black men and women would say amen to that, and probably a lot of our bruised White brothers too.

Now let's just imagine for a moment the consequences of America's spiritual leaders aggressively and routinely incorporating the theology of the Prophet Amos into their sermons.

I've got to admit, a part of me would love to be in the affluent American church that one day gets enough nerve to adequately confront the heartlessness of the rich, the lack of justice for the righteous and the emptiness of religious ritual without true faith.

I'm betting their survival rates would be directly proportional to the degree of emphasis they put upon these subjects.

The next Prophet who stood out for me as being more meaningful for America today was **Isaiah.**

Isaiah caught my attention primarily because he refused to diminish or minimize the hypocrisy of the leaders in his day.

After reading Isaiah, I came to sense a very desperate need for his influence in the mainstream American church in particular. Doesn't somebody clearly need to tell this country's congregations, thus says the LORD ...

> I am sick and tired of your meaningless conventions. Don't bring me any more of your prayer vigils.

> Why do you keep parading around broadcasting your worthless efforts?

> I'm not interested in the latest Christian video or CD, and your idea of what I look like stinks.

> Your holidays and festivals ... they are all sinful and false. I want nothing to do with them.

> I hate all your celebrations and sanctimonious gatherings. " I cannot stand the sight of them.

> From now on when you lift your hands in prayer, I will refuse to look.

> Even though you offer many prayers, I will not listen. For your hands are covered with the blood of your innocent victims.

> Wash yourselves and be clean!
> Let me no longer see your evil deeds.
> Give up your wicked ways.
> Learn to do good.

> Seek justice.
> Help the oppressed.
> Defend the orphan.
> Fight for the rights of widows."

Isaiah 1:1-17

Yet another significant reason why Isaiah stood out for me personally was that he emphasized an additional shortcoming in American theology I was previously unaware of until I read his book for myself:

The diminished fear and respect for the LORD'S judgment and discipline.

Let me tell you something. God is no joke. And there is no way in the world anyone in their right mind can read His Word and not know this.

Although God's disciplinary actions seem rather extreme by today's standards, it's only because Western Christianity has failed to underscore and convey the extremely horrific, degrading and contagious nature of sin.

Sin and hell are no joke either.

In chapter 2, Isaiah expands upon one scenario in particular that provoked God to respond with punishment and correction:

> The people bow down and worship these things they have made.
>
> So now everyone will be humbled and brought low.
> The LORD simply cannot ignore their sins.
>
> Crawl into caves in the rocks.
>
> Hide from the terror of the LORD and the glory of His Majesty.
>
> The day is coming when your pride will be brought low and the LORD alone will be exalted.
>
> In that day the LORD Almighty will punish the proud, bringing them down to the dust.

Now if we don't think God will respond to America's idolatry and pride in the very same way or worse (because they should know better) then we've been victimized by Western Christianity.

And finally, in chapter 58, Isaiah offers some extremely valuable and relevant insight for many of America's self-professed contemporary Christians.

You seem eager to learn His teachings.

You act like a nation that wants to do right by obeying His laws.

You ask Him about justice and say you enjoy worshiping the LORD.

You wonder why the LORD pays no attention when you fast and act humble.

But on those same days that you fast, you think only of yourselves and abuse your workers.

You even get angry and ready to fight.

I'll tell you what it really means to worship the LORD.

Remove the chains of prisoners who are chained unjustly. Free those who are abused!

Share your food with everyone who is hungry; share your home with the poor and homeless.

Give clothes to those in need; don't turn away your relatives.

But I can hear American Christians right now, moaning and groaning, "We can't possibly do all of these things in contemporary society. Are you crazy? Besides, that's all Old Testament religion anyway."

Well, that's exactly what I would expect from them. Anything to assist in exempting and excluding them from actually Doing What Jesus Would Do.

That's why morality in America is a big joke.

The next Prophet that I found to be more relevant for contemporary American society would be **Micah,** because of his bold confrontation and incrimination of the greedy people in his day.

Will there be no end of your getting rich by cheating?

> The homes of the wicked are filled with treasures
> gained by dishonestly measuring out grain in short measures.
>
> And how can I tolerate all your merchants who use dishonest scales and weights?
>
> The rich among you have become wealthy though extortion and violence.
>
> Your citizens are so used to lying that their tongues can no longer tell the truth.
>
> Therefore ... you will eat but never have enough. Your hunger pangs and emptiness will remain.
>
> And though you try to save your money, it will come to nothing in the end.
>
> You will save a little, but I will give it to those who conquer you.
>
> You will plant crops but not harvest them..."
>
> *Micah 6:10-15*

Wow! I bet the Native Americans would say amen to this.

However, here in America, where "the lifestyles of the rich and famous" are routinely emphasized and idolized, the extreme financial disparity that exists is hardly ever questioned or investigated.

And what's worse, is that almost everyone who endorses it also refuses to even consider the possibility that there could be a better way to live, or that there might be any negative aspects to this financial ethic.

Personally, I don't see how anyone could ever fully grasp it and not wind up sick to their stomach.

The amount of waste generated by this country alone is criminal by itself, but in light of the fact that there are still millions of malnourished and starving human beings on this planet, it is inhuman and barbaric.

America's experts and scholars can praise, promote and justify this financial ethic all they want to, but its fruits keep becoming clearer and clearer everyday, don't they?

Today's Americans are not only the fattest and most in-debt generation ever, but they're also best described as a generation that would do anything for money and power.

Boy isn't America advanced!

In the verses quoted above, the allusion to grain of course applies to any commodity or service that's sold at a disproportionate profit margin. But then, just what is disproportionate?

Well, rather than attempt to define the term (which is how the expert advocates of this financial ethic legitimize it and minimize its horror) I'll simply challenge each and every individual who considers themselves to be ethical and open-minded to objectively investigate the other side of this economic system for themselves. [9]

Otherwise you're simply mimicking someone elses ethic, values and outlook again, and they call that a puppet, not a citizen.

The next Prophet I found to be more significant for modern America tums out to be **Zephaniah**, because of his focus upon the spiritual infidelity in his day.

From an African-American perspective that would of course compare with our betrayal of a faith and belief that delivered us through the most abominable predicament human beings have ever known, with minimal violence (legalized slavery, lynching and discrimination).

And after prevailing over this appalling predicament by relying upon this overcoming faith, who did we turn to for further blessings?

Well, for one, we turned to Louis Farrakhan and his Black Muslims, didn't we?

We also turned to astrology; the sun, the moon and the stars. And then there was Buddhism, Mormonism, Scientology and even Secular Humanism, which are all nothing but one uninspired individual's organized response to a compromised, false and mingled Christianity.

Well, aren't we a lot like the Jews.

Zephaniah also re-condemns the injustice and arrogance of God's people (which are Jews and Christians today), he re-affirms the Day of Judgment, (which is coming) and then re-issues a plea for repentance, humility, righteousness and obedience.

Finally Zephaniah concludes his oracle with a statement that once meant so much to us back in the day. Back during a time when we collectively understood our identity, destiny and relevance from a Biblical perspective:

> "From across the rivers of Ethiopia, my scattered people, my true worshippers, will bring offerings to me."

The next Prophet to deliver an especially relevant message for contemporary African-Americans would be **Jeremiah.**

As I was reading his book, I came across a slew of significant principles that would have certainly bore repeating here if time and space permitted, however, once I arrived at chapter 12, I was compelled to stop and acknowledge the significance of Jeremiah's age old question for Black people in America.

> God!!! "Why are the wicked so prosperous? And why are evil people so happy?"

The next Prophet who stood out for me was **Habakkuk,** because the first two chapters of his book are simply tailor-made for this self-professed Christian country.

Habakkuk, much like many other authentic believers in America today finds himself getting extremely fed up with enduring all the violence, crime, cruelty and injustice among his people, so he begins to ask God for help.

And God responds with an answer that Habakkuk can hardly believe. He tells Habakkuk He's going to send a very advanced yet wicked nation to discipline His people.

Habakkuk responds by complaining to God that His people are helpless against this evil nation and that they will become their captives and help make them rich.

God responds by repeating His demands for His people's lifestyle and culture and the consequences of betraying Him.

He then goes on to elaborate upon some of the more specific things that provoked Him to discipline them.

> Look at the proud!
>
> They trust in themselves, and their lives are crooked ...
>
> Wealth is treacherous, and the arrogant are never at rest.
>
> They range far and wide, with their mouths opened as wide as death, but they are never satisfied.
>
> In their greed they have gathered up many nations and peoples.
>
> But the time is coming when all their captives will taunt them, saying, "You thieves! At last justice has caught up with you!
>
> Now you will get what you deserve for your oppression and extortion!"

Suddenly, your debtors will rise up in anger. They will turn on you and take all you have, while you stand trembling and helpless.

You have plundered many nations; now they will plunder you. You murderers!

You have filled the countryside with violence and all the cities, too.

"How terrible it will be for you who get rich by unjust means!

You believe your wealth will buy security, putting your families beyond the reach of danger.

But by the murders you committed, you have shamed your name and forfeited your lives.

The very stones in the walls of your houses cry out against you, and the beams in the ceilings echo the complaint.

"How terrible it will be for you who build cities with money gained by murder and corruption!

Has not the LORD Almighty promised that the wealth of nations will turn to ashes?

They work so hard, but all in vain!

"How terrible it will be for you who make your neighbors drunk!

You force your cup on them so that you can gloat over their nakedness and shame.

But soon it will be your turn! Come, drink and be exposed!

Drink from the cup of the LORD's judgment, and all your glory will be turned to shame.

You cut down the forests of Lebanon. Now you will be cut down!

You terrified the wild animals you caught in your traps. Now terror will strike you because of your murder and violence in cities everywhere!

"What have you gained by worshiping all your man-made idols?

How foolish to trust in something made by your own hands! What fools you are to believe such lies!

How terrible it will be for you who beg lifeless wooden idols to save you.

You ask speechless stone images to tell you what to do. Can an idol speak for God?

They may be overlaid with gold and silver, but they are lifeless inside.

I also found it interesting that the LORD told Habakkuk His discipline would not happen right away, but *"Slowly, steadily, surely ..."*

He said, *"If it seems slow, wait patiently,* for it will surely take place. It will not be delayed."

Habakkuk concludes his prophecy by reminiscing upon the goodness and the awesomeness of God and the success of His ways throughout the history of His people. The final verses of his book bear repeating.

"Though the fig tree may not blossom,
Nor fruit be on the vines;
though the labor of the olive may fail,
and the fields yield no food;
though the flock may be cut off from the fold,
and there be no herd in the stalls —
yet will I rejoice in the LORD,

I will joy in the God of my salvation."

Now if you ask me, that's nothing less than authentic, Biblical Christianity.

Yet another Prophet that I couldn't help but appreciate as a Christian in modern America was **Ezekiel.**

Even though Ezekiel is one of many Prophets who were inspired to identify and highlight the significant damage that a bad shepherd does to the great plan of God, his particular condemnation is still one that stood out for me personally.

In chapter 34, Ezekiel starts out by recalling some of the specific behaviors and consequences of bad shepherds or leaders, whether they were spiritual or secular.

As a consequence of all the bad shepherding in Ezekiel's time, God had not only resolved to take care of His own sheep, or His own people, but He had also decided to declare judgment upon the fat and the strong sheep, or the people who were doggin' out the weak sheep.

Now I can't help but believe that if all the people who've ever been frustrated by America's no-good religious leaders knew that the God of the Bible blames these bad shepherds for the sad condition of His church today, it just might make a difference.

Consequently, I no longer fault the typical mainstream American Christian for being so arrogant, aggressive, superficial and loose, because their leaders are frequently arrogant, aggressive, superficial and loose.

Nor do I blame the typical mainstream American Christian for being so stingy with their illegitimate wealth, because their leaders are typically stingy with theirs.

I've come to realize that mainstream American "Christians" are a happy and deceived bunch because their leaders are typically deceived and happy.

And evidently I'm not the only one who believes this. One of the more popular reasons people do not attend church anymore is because they've come to realize that their spiritual leaders are far too often hypocrites.

Last but not least is the Prophet **Daniel.**

Now although Daniel wrote primarily concerning his own personal predicament there in Babylon, I was still able to glean a lot from him and his three compatriots who were all shown favor by the Babylonians during their Captivity.

Perhaps the most important lesson was that Daniel and his friends were not overcome by any national allegiances or creeds in order to be true to their God.

The Jehovah's Witnesses and a few others are bold enough to follow his example.

However, the mainstream American church not only has no shame in this area, but is actually proud to pledge allegiance, and will kick your butt if you aren't too!

So now you know why American ministers don't teach the whole Bible in their churches.

Sixteen different Prophets wrote sixteen different books, mainly warning (the Jews) against social, economic, spiritual and political exploitation, oppression and infidelity, and they all make up one full quarter of the Bible's sixty-six books.

Quite obviously America's Bible experts have not been exposing their gullible congregations to this part of the Book to the same degree as the other three quarters.

Instead they have placed major emphasis upon the New Testament, which is a little less than half the whole Bible, and this has caused a very important part of God's Word to go neglected.

It isn't coincidental either that this neglected division of God's

Word containing an abundance of lessons, messages, examples, criticisms and warnings to the nations and the leaders has been disregarded.

Coincidences on this scale don't exist.

Ultimately, if this country is ever going to last and tap into its true potential, the Prophets must be given equal attention and perhaps even more.

America had better learn as quickly as Nineveh, that economic and social exploitation, oppression and injustice will not work forever.

And its church had better learn just as quick that any theology encouraging its followers to focus only on themselves and their natural, never-ending shortcomings rather than those *outside forces* that stroke and inspire the shortcomings also, *is demonic.*

Such a theology is in bed with "the world". And it has America's congregations unknowingly *allied* with a culture that teases and tempts them at every turn while they fight the never-ending battle with the flesh.

For societies like America that are being relentlessly bombarded with sensually targeted distractions and traps, these Prophetic messages and warnings are more than just relevant, they're mandatory.

Ignoring them is what eventually led to the downfall of God's own Chosen!

How many of us can see the downfall of this kingdom occurring?

As I've heard one legitimate spiritual leader say so many times, "as goes the spiritual or moral leadership of a nation, so goes the nation".

It was only a matter of time before the affluence attained by the Jews in Babylon changed their collective character into the one that became the target of so many nations thereafter (if you know their history from then on).

How many of us can see a change in the collective character of Black people in America?

The second and supporting resource that our legitimate spiritual leaders must start aggressively and routinely incorporating into their theology is those divinely inspired, pioneering Black ministers who once, by faith, put life, limb and loved ones on the line in order to emphasize Biblical themes of heritage, oppression, liberation, love, and justice in their studies and sermons.

They knew early on that our identity and culture had suffered as a consequence of our coerced assimilation. This would include such men and works as:

Rev. Lemuel Haynes (1753)
"Black Preacher to White America: The Collected Writings of Lemuel Haynes, 1774-1833"

Rev. Absolom Jones (1746)
"Thanksgiving Sermon"

Bishop Richard Allen (1760)
"The Life, Experience, and Gospel Labours of the Rt. Rev. Richard Allen"

Rev. James William Charles Pennington, D.D. (1807)
"Text Book of the Origin and History of the Colored People"

Bishop Daniel Alexander Payne (1811)
"Sermons and Addresses"

Bishop James Theodore Holly (1829)
"The Divine Plan of Human Redemption in Its Ethnological Development"

Bishop Henry McNeil Turner (1834)
"God is a Negro"

Rev. Rufus L. Perry, PH.D. (1834)
"The Cushite, or the Children of Ham as seen by the Ancient Historians and Poets"

Rev. Francis J. Grimke (1850)
"Works of Francis James Grimke"

Bishop Lucius Hosley (18XX)
"Autobiography, Sermons, Addresses and Essays"

Bishop Reverdy Ransom (1861)
"Making the Gospel Plain: The Writings of Bishop Reverdy Ransom (African American Religious Thought)"

Dr. Howard Thurman (1900)
"Jesus and the Disinherited"

Father Gustavo Gutierrez (1928)
"A Theology of Liberation"

Rev. Doctor Martin Luther King Jr. (1929)
"Strength to Love"

Professor James H. Cone (1945)
"Risks of Faith: The Emergence of a Black Theology of Liberation, 1968-1998"

Rev. Doctor Allan Aubrey Boesak (1945)
"Farewell to Innocence"

Bishop Manas Buthelezi (19XX)
"The Relevance of Black Theology"

Dr. John S. Mbiti (19XX)
"Bible and Theology in African Christianity"

This list is by no means comprehensive, but rather a mere sampling of all the great resources available to any pastor who is serious about ministering to a people who've been victimized by compromised and mingled American Christianity.

Had Black ministers in America possessed the nerve and independence to fully embrace and develop the rudimentary theology of men like these when it was initially introduced, this present generation of African-Americans would very likely be enjoying a much better church and country today.

Even though some of these theologians did indeed go a bit overboard in re-evaluating certain aspects of the Bible for their people, they were nevertheless standing alone on very new ground as they did so.

Those legitimate aspects of Western theology certainly didn't pop into existence fully polished either, did they? For that matter, neither did authentic Christian theology during the first century.

Our Bible scholars cracked open the very same Bible, discovered the very same Salvation and Doctrine, but came up with a very different Jesus.

First of all, the Jesus we discovered was not a good-looking, feminine White man with long, straight or blond or brunette hair.

According to the Prophets John and Daniel, He was a man of color with thick, woolly hair. And in keeping with Paul's testimony, His hair must have been short since it was disgraceful for a man to wear his hair long in that day.

Isaiah portrayed the LORD prophetically as possessing no form, comeliness or beauty that anyone should desire Him.

The Jesus we discovered didn't identify with our racist oppressors either. Nor did He forgive them freely for their atrocities or make excuses for their ignorance.

He was said to be Himself, oppressed and afflicted, despised and rejected by men, and a man of sorrows, acquainted with grief.

And finally, the Jesus we discovered didn't speak metaphorically when He declared His purpose in the world.

> The Spirit of the LORD is upon Me, because He has anointed Me to preach the gospel to the poor;

> He has sent Me to heal the brokenhearted, to proclaim liberty to the captives and recovery of sight to the blind, to set at liberty those who are oppressed...

> *(Isaiah 61:1)*

Now this is a Jesus who transcends race and class, and this is a theology that rises above national and political allegiances.

It avoids the arrogance of mainstream interpretations, by emphasizing and highlighting a Biblical Jesus rather than a "made in America" Jesus whom most Christians seem to simply *"feel"*.

This is also a consistent and legitimate Jesus who not only identifies with the poor and the oppressed, but also helps lead them towards a legitimate freedom.

He has fixed the unfixable, and changed the unchangeable.

Do you know Him?

Standards

Every Black person in America should know by now that we cannot progress collectively by embracing several different standards. If we aspire to advance as individuals, we can. If we are islands, we can, and many of us have already.

However, collectively, Black people in America cannot afford to be islands. Nor have we ever attempted to be, until here recently anyway.

We've always been a community-oriented people, and we have always embraced a Standard we perceived to be pre-established by an impartial, ethical, loving, all-knowing and all-powerful Creator of all things.

Consequently, contrary to popular opinion, it wasn't the White man's God, Bible or religion that our ancestors and forefathers chose to embrace, respect and follow.

It was the liberating, fair and mighty God who had been revealed in the Bible along with His exceptional Son.

And as Rev. Burrough always said, "if the White man did change the Bible, he sure did a poor job."

Black Bible critics have forgotten that it was the God who planted mankind in Africa and then declared that one day His scattered people, His true worshippers across Ethiopia's rivers, would bring Him offerings that our ancestors and forefathers embraced.

The increased scrutiny of this inimitable Book and its historical narratives by today's Black Americans has only been a recent occurrence. Most everyone else around the world still readily acknowledges that embracing its principles and standards was the right thing for us to have done.

Undoubtedly, it was the inspiration for many a callous and arrogant American heart and mind changing. It loosened the grip they had on our throats and set the stage for a peaceful co-existence with them (a forced peace at least).

It also set the stage for our accelerated advancement among them (albeit with a glass ceiling).

Contrast our past with many other societies and you will start to acquire a deeper appreciation for how effective our Standard was.

Black folk here in America changed the world when we took the higher ground and demanded the American Pharaohs submit to that which was right and good. Their standard did not motivate them to collectively initiate such a change nor to support it.

Those Black slave preachers who hadn't assimilated were not ignorant. If books like "Black Religion and Black Radicalism" by Gayraud Wilmore had been included in Black church curricula long ago, we'd all possess a much deeper appreciation for the Biblical standards they employed to overcome our enslavement by now.

For those of us who wish to remain in the past and continue to believe that Bible-based religion is the White man's religion or that he changed the Bible, it's time for you to wise up.

While it's absolutely true that certain versions and interpretations of particular Biblical principles and texts handed down to us here in America were indeed manipulated and corrupted, that's now ancient history.

When someone misuses something against you, you don't just write the thing off altogether.

Some bad air shouldn't cause you to stop breathing. Some bad relationships shouldn't cause you to write the opposite sex off, and some bad preachers or false Christians misusing the Bible shouldn't cause you to disregard the church or the Book altogether.

Rather than being disregarded or mocked, each and every pioneering Black preacher who refused to either ignore or counteract that wonder-working, over-coming and hope-filled Book back then, deserves to be celebrated and honored today.

Had they not stood their ground and uncovered the Bible's emphasis upon liberation, love and justice, the Civil Rights era most likely would've never occurred.

Unfortunately however, by the time they did finally begin to challenge the American church leaders with this authentic theology, the church leaders were so absorbed with blessing the powers that be that they couldn't perceive the legitimacy of our theologians' claims. [10]

It didn't seem to matter that our theologians confronted the church leaders according to the Biblical Standard. They were all either ignored, given token attention or assimilated into the mainstream.

But that didn't deter them all.

A few of our more dedicated, unassimilated and independent thinking Black theologians stood their ground and ultimately wrestled Christianity away from that old Western stronghold that had generated and supported corrupt power, greed and arrogance.

Western Christianity, if we can call it that, had not been capable of generating a Civil Rights movement for Black people in America or an Anti-Apartheid movement for Black Africans in South Africa. Western "Christianity" could not have helped the Brown Christians in South America or the White Christians in Eastern Europe either.

Western "Christianity" had demanded, promoted and produced blind obedience, arrogance, bondage, hypocrisy, deceit and exclusion.

Real Christianity on the other hand demands, promotes and produces real justice, freedom, peace, love and brotherhood.

This is therefore the Standard we need to re-embrace.

It is the original Standard for all mankind and every other standard is nothing more than one man's corrupted hand-me-down of it or supplement to it.

Over and over again, its authenticity has been confirmed in numerous different ways and it has never been disproven.

Given all the evidence outlined in Josh McDowell's book, "Evidence That Demands a Verdict", any great skeptic with a lick of sense would conclude likewise.

According to McDowell, the Bible is the only book that was:

> Written over about a fifteen hundred year span. Written on three different continents, including Asia, Africa and Europe. And written in three different languages, including Hebrew, Aramaic and Greek.

> It was written by more than forty authors from every walk of life, including kings, military leaders, peasants, philosophers, fishermen, tax collectors, poets, musicians, statesmen, scholars and shepherds.

> And written in a variety of literary styles, including poetry, historical narrative, song, romance, didactic treatise, personal correspondence, memoirs, satire, biography, autobiography, law, prophecy, parable, and allegory.

> The Bible addresses hundreds of controversial subjects from Genesis to Revelation, including marriage, divorce, remarriage, homosexuality, adultery, obedience to authority,

truth-telling and lying, character development, parenting, the nature and revelation of God, with an amazing degree of harmony.

And in spite of the Bible's diversity, it presents a single unfolding story: God's redemption of human beings. Among all the people described in the Bible, the leading character throughout is the one, true living God made known through Jesus Christ.

And if all that weren't enough, what really impressed me the most as a feeble, undependable, weak, foolish and sometimes ridiculous human being who's unworthy of identifying with the people God used to establish His Standard or being used myself by the all-mighty God, is that they were all for the most part, just as fickle and undeserving as me.

Abraham was a liar

Jacob was a liar

Joseph was abused

Judah was a drunk

Moses had a stuttering problem

Gideon was afraid

Samson had long hair and was a womanizer

Rahab was a prostitute

Jeremiah and Timothy were too young

David had an affair and was a murderer

Elijah was suicidal

Isaiah preached naked

Jonah ran from God

Naomi was a widow

Job went bankrupt

John the Baptist ate bugs

Peter denied Christ

> The Disciples fell asleep while praying
>
> Martha worried about everything
>
> The Samaritan woman was divorced, many times
>
> Zaccheus was too small
>
> Paul was too religious
>
> Timothy had an ulcer, and
>
> Lazarus was dead

Collectively, Black people in America today have even more reason to embrace this exceptional Book considering the fruits being enjoyed by this new generation.

In fact, the validity of a Biblical Standard should be unquestionable for us by now. Black critics of its strategy enjoy that freedom at the expense of its martyrs.

However the Civil Rights Movement got the attention and respect of the entire world, didn't it? Oppressed people around the globe still copy its strategy, and whether we know it or not, it was a Biblical movement that put us ahead by leap years.

It's what gave our Grandmas and Grandpas the courage and strength to rise up and toss that monster off our backs.

Believe you me, nothing else inspired us to rise to great levels of achievement after suffering through the longest period in history of the most inhuman treatment human beings have ever received.

We should be nearly extinct, just like this country's natives.

Yet some of us rise.

Don't fool yourself. We collectively put our faith and trust in a Standard we knew would work. Dr. King may have led it, but we embraced it because in our souls we knew it was right.

Even though we do indeed possess many legitimate complaints concerning the present state of the American church and its spiritual leaders today, many of the spiritual leaders in Jesus' day were also either inadequate or corrupt, weren't they?

And although many of them compromised God's Word as well, Jesus Himself still attended a synagogue, didn't He? Ever wonder why Jesus would still routinely attend God's House in spite of this?

Because He knew they weren't all corrupt!

Therefore, Christ left us the example of a committed temple attender who was passionately involved in God's house and business, and not that of an uninvolved critic

He knew that every uninvolved critic, not contributing to the restoration and strengthening of the church was essentially contributing to:

> More gruesome brutalities
>
> Increased sexual perversion and deviation
>
> More destroyed families
>
> More crack babies
>
> More aborted babies
>
> More hopelessness, abuse, neglect, etc.

In other words, the LORD knew that the Church was designed to maintain the Standard.

Here in America however, His Church and Standard has been seriously Westernized, much like the Jewish practice of their faith was Hellenized by the Greek culture they assimilated into later.

Consequently, many contemporary Americans have mistakenly assumed that the Church has to evolve like other Western institutions.

The Church however is not a man-made institution. It was designed by God. The same God who designed the body and the family.

And contrary to popular opinion, the pope, the president, the scientist or the king cannot legitimately modify God's creations without inducing some sorts of long-term negative effects.

No human being can legitimately upgrade, enhance or renovate the design of the church, the body or the family. They will always function best when operated in accordance to the designer's specifications and there's no way around that.

So, it shouldn't surprise anyone that a "properly working" church is one that operates as closely to the original model as possible.

Now let's just imagine for a moment if you can, American Christians finally starting to take the original church model and design more seriously.

It's not impossible, nor is it ridiculous. And it isn't like people would have to start wearing robes and sandals again.

All we really have to do is restore the lost art of Agape and Koinonia ... concepts that are embodied in the following verses:

> "All the LORD'S followers often met together, and they shared everything they had. They would sell their property and possessions and give the money to whoever needed it. Day after day they met together in the temple.

> They broke bread together in different homes and shared their food happily and freely, while praising God. Everyone liked them, and each day the LORD added to their group others who were being saved."

> *Acts 2:44-47 (NKJV)*

Now anyone who calls themselves a Christian but can't fully embrace this basic concept of the Creator's beloved community has been victimized by compromised American Christianity.

Anyone who can't wholeheartedly buy into this beloved community as an absolute, literal reality to be fought for here on earth and not compromised, has been misled by their minister.

And if a few of the mature believers in each neighborhood can't convince a handful of their neighbors to participate in periodic block-parties, then they've been ill-equipped by him as well. Getting people together to share a meal and enjoy inspiring conversations isn't rocket science.

Agape-feasts were designed to engender and advance the Biblical principles of goodwill, brotherly love and fellowship in any community, and that induces a love for our faith by example.

And whenever there was any arrogance or division within them, group leaders put it in check with a quickness.

Koinonia is nothing more than the intentional and purposeful sharing of a Christian's time, talents, and treasures with each other and their neighbors.

Interestingly enough, according to the Wikipedia website, "As class distinctions became set in the early church, the Agape Feast began to fall out of favor."

This is a situation that has to be changed by real Christians. We must start acting more like the spiritual hospital for each other and our neighbors rather than the morality police.

This is what helped ignite the amazing growth of the first church!

Neighborhood churches like these, led by anointed believers of the Gospel would certainly spark some significant changes in this country.

Black Christian communities could focus upon injustices and oppression within their precincts, while integrated Christian neighborhoods could focus upon the degree of racial unity within theirs.

White Christian neighborhoods could of course focus upon humility, truth, justice and equality.

And before long, there would be a lot less of these segregated neighborhoods ... *thanks to God!*

Any approach implemented to make the church be the church will fail unless it's designed to revive the original model.

And the original model is only impractical if you haven't been a victim of this immoral and unjust culture.

Allegiances

During an interview on Sept 13th, 2001 (two days after 9-11) with Jane Clayson, the CBS Early Show host, the daughter of Billy Graham, Anne Graham Lotz stated:

> "I would also say for several years now Americans in a sense have shaken their fist at God and said, God, we want you out of our schools, our government, our business, we want you out of our marketplace. And God, who is a gentleman, has just quietly backed out of our national and political life, our public life, removing his hand of blessing and protection."

> "We need to turn to God first of all and say, God, we're sorry we have treated you this way and we invite you now to come into our national life. We put our trust in you. We have our trust in God on our coins, we need to practice it" (*Lotz*).

The following excerpt, although specifically referring to 9-11, provides an additional prophetic look into *the real relationship America has with God.*

Anyone who sees it differently is only deceiving themselves. You can't just live any way you want to and expect the God of the Bible to "shed His grace on thee".

Pastor Joe Wright, in his opening prayer on January 23, 1996 for the Kansas House of Representatives, also offers a prophetic look at the real relationship that America has with the God of the Bible.

Heavenly Father, we come before you today to ask your

forgiveness and seek your direction and guidance. We know your Word says, "Woe to those who call evil good," but that's exactly what we've done. We have lost our spiritual equilibrium and inverted our values.

We confess that we have ridiculed the absolute truth of your Word and called it moral pluralism. We have worshipped other gods and called it multiculturalism. We have endorsed perversion and called it an alternative lifestyle.

We have exploited the poor and called it the lottery. We have neglected the needy and called it self-preservation. We have rewarded laziness and called it welfare. We have killed our unborn and called it choice. We have shot abortionists and called it justifiable.

We have neglected to discipline our children and called it building esteem. We have abused power and called it political savvy. We have coveted our neighbor's possessions and called it ambition. We have polluted the air with profanity and pornography and called it freedom of expression.

We have ridiculed the time-honored values of our forefathers and called it enlightenment. Search us O God and know our hearts today; try us and see if there be some wicked way in us; cleanse us from every sin and set us free.

Guide and bless these men and women who have been sent here by the people of Kansas, and who have been ordained by you, to govern this great state. Grant them your wisdom to rule and may their decisions direct us to the center of your will. I ask it in the name of your Son, the living Savior, Jesus Christ.

Amen *(Wright).*

Anne Graham Lotz only sees America as shaking its fist at God for "several years", but we know better. From its very foundation, as judged by its actions (fruits), this country has been:

> The chief hypocrite.
> Just ask the American Indians.
>
> The chief murderer.
> Just ask Amnesty International.
>
> The chief extortionist.
> Just ask the Third World.
>
> The chief pervert.
> America is pornography central.

Once I started connecting all the dark dots in American culture and history, I couldn't help but wonder ... was it really God who shed His Grace on this nation to make it so "great"?

Or could it have been the free blood, sweat and tears of our ancestors? Could it's "greatness" have come as a consequence of the sacrificed lives of the natives (with whom they broke every treaty)?

Or could it have been through the arrogance of believing God ordained its rise to power (Manifest Destiny)? Maybe it was through the treachery of its trade practices. [11]

And if it was, did I really want to pledge allegiance to an overly aggressive and arrogant country that has strong-armed its way to the top? Will that country ever have any real allies or any real peace?

Can anyone ever really trust them? Are they really admired or respected? Or are people only envying their stolen possessions and illegitimate power because they have a hidden agenda?

Bullies are always paranoid and insecure, because they know that the people they've strong-armed on their way to the so-called "top" have perfect reason to turn on them.

So do I really want to pledge allegiance to that kind of country??

Personally, when I choose where to place my allegiance, I also take time to study what the critics have to say.

In this case I went to a person whose analysis of this culture and country has withstood the test of time: Professor Howard Zinn. Professor Zinn has taught history and political science at Spelman College in Atlanta and at Boston University, where he was Professor Emeritus.

He is the author of, "A People's History of the United States", and an Amazon reviewer wrote this concerning his book:

> "Howard Zinn infuses the often-submerged voices of Blacks, women, American Indians, war resisters, and poor laborers of all nationalities into this thorough narrative that spans American history from Christopher Columbus's arrival to an after word on the Clinton presidency.

> Addressing his trademark reversals of perspective, Zinn—a teacher, historian, and social activist for more than 20 years —explains, "My point is not that we must, in telling history, accuse, judge, condemn Columbus in absentia. It is too late for that; it would be a useless scholarly exercise in morality.

> But the easy acceptance of atrocities as a deplorable but necessary price to pay for progress (Hiroshima and Vietnam, to save Western civilization; Kronstadt and Hungary, to save socialism; nuclear proliferation, to save us all)—that is still with us.

> One reason these atrocities are still with us is that we have learned to bury them in a mass of other facts, as radioactive wastes are buried in containers in the earth."

If your last experience of American history was brought to you by junior high school textbooks—or even if you're a specialist—get ready for the other side of stories you may not even have heard.

With its vivid descriptions of rarely noted events, A People's History of the United States is required reading for anyone who wants to take a fresh look at the rich, rocky history of America (Amazon.com).[12]

Other easily accepted atrocities that are still with us buried beneath a mass of other facts, include Black slavery, rape, genocide, exploitation, perversion, etc.

All of this history must be considered as well when it comes to fairly and properly measuring this country's true culture before we can soberly place our allegiances.

Then, we must not only consider the negative deeds of a nation in our measurements, but we've also got to consider the fluff. By fluff, I mean the rhetoric and the ideology.

Every nation thinks and speaks highly of itself, doesn't it? They all possess great slogans, mottoes and creeds, don't they? But they cannot all be as great as they say or think they are, can they?

That's why it's extremely important we apply a Biblical Standard in our judgment of cultures.

All of the patriotic propaganda has to be ignored and the goodness and badness or rightness and wrongness of a culture must be measured strictly by evaluating its roots and its fruits. Regarding a society's roots, the Bible declares:

> "Seeds that fall on rocky ground are people who gladly hear the message and accept it. But they don't have deep roots and they believe only for a little while. As soon as life gets hard, they give up.
>
> Seeds that fall among the thorn bushes are also people who hear the message [they also have roots]. But they are so eager for riches and pleasures that they never produce anything."
>
> *Luke 8:13 and 14 (CEV)*

Concerning a society's fruits, the Bible warns:

> "Watch out for false prophets! They dress up like sheep, but inside they are wolves who have come to attack you. You can

tell what they are by what they do. No one picks grapes or figs from thorn bushes. A good tree produces good fruit, and a bad tree produces bad fruit.

A good tree cannot produce bad fruit, and a bad tree cannot produce good fruit. Every tree that produces bad fruit will be chopped down and burned. You can tell who the false prophets are by their deeds."

Matthew 7:15:20 (CEV)

Not By Their Words! Not By Their Constitutions, Declarations or Pledges!

That being said, it should be rather obvious by now that there's an awful lot of rotten fruit growing on the American tree.

In fact, when I reflect upon the fruits of this American nation, I can't help but be reminded of the stirring lyrics of a song made famous by Billie Holiday in 1939: Strange Fruit. [13]

Southern trees bear a strange fruit
blood on the leaves and blood at the root

Black body swinging in the southern breeze
strange fruit hanging from the poplar trees

Pastoral scene of the gallant south
the bulging eyes and the twisted mouth

Scent of magnolia sweet and fresh
and the sudden smell of burning flesh!

Here is a fruit for the crows to pluck
for the rain to gather, for the wind to suck

For the sun to rot, for a tree to drop
here is a strange and bitter crop (Meeropol).

Is additional evidence confirming the rotten roots and fruit of this country required?

Can you think of any stronger resistance to the Christian faith today than the past actions of the American church and its European ancestor? Including their involvement in:

African Slavery

Native American Genocide

World Colonization

Racism

Crusades

Secret Societies

The Inquisition

The Holocaust

Hiroshima

Vietnam

The so-called American Christians place "In God we trust" on the same money they place secret occult symbols upon!

What god do they trust in??

It *can't be* the one in the Bible!

Their founding fathers were knee-deep into the occult. No wonder they couldn't see the actual evils they perpetuated *(Sutton 113, 142, 145)*.

And now, the Mormons want to resurrect that same blending of the occult and Christianity *(Brooke)*. They better read the real Word of God and toss that other piece of garbage.

And speaking of people who blend Christianity with other evil things, check out the so-called moral President's involvement in the secret society known as "Skull and Bones" *(Geo. W Bush)*

An Internet search on this subject will reveal some very shaky things about this hypocrite. Moral Christian President my eye! Last time I checked, the skull and bones insignia was a symbol for poison. Indeed!

The so-called "Protestant Reformation", which American Christians hold in such high esteem, completely ignored the slavery issue.

And little more than 400 years later, the same country that experienced this so-called, great religious movement was exterminating Europe's Jews, while its reformed and enlightened church did nothing!

America's "Christian" festivals are founded upon the worship of heathen deities (Easter, Christmas, etc.) and the days of their week are named after heathen deities (Moon Day, Saturn Day, Thor's Day, Sun Day, etc.).

They perpetuate, even to this day, a corrupted image of the Christ. And in spite of the dangers of image worship, they perpetuate images that have no historic or cultural basis, but are instead arrogant caricatures of a deceived American church.

No wonder a new religion pops up daily in this country.

What else?

They perpetuate even to this day, a racially divided church. Sunday morning is still the most segregated moment in America, isn't it??

And on top of all that, when it comes to charity they're hypocrites as well!

"Christian America's" true giving habits are exposed in a book entitled, "Rich Christians in an Age of Hunger: A Biblical Study", by Ronald J. Sider.

In the section entitled "How Generous Are We?" Sider writes,

> "The U.S. is the richest nation in the world. But the data [...] reveals that the U.S. government ranks fifth from the bottom [...] among the major Western donors of foreign aid."

> "Popular opinion does not reflect this reality. A recent survey discovered that more than two-thirds (69%) of all Americans think that the U.S. is more generous in foreign aid than other developed nations. Perhaps our illusion of generosity is a necessary protective device. In order to justify our affluence, we foster an image of generous nation dispensing foreign aid on a grand scale." *(Sider 50)*.

How could it be otherwise when the most influential economist of this century was an aristocratic and irreligious sodomite with the gall to proclaim:

> "For at least another hundred years, we must pretend to

> ourselves and to everyone that fair is foul and foul is fair: for foul is useful and fair is not. Avarice and usury and precaution must be our gods for a little longer still. For only they can lead us out of the tunnel of economic necessity into daylight." [14]

America's "Christians" see so clearly the deceit [15] and oppression [16] in every other country, but when it comes to seeing any in its own, it appears to be deaf, dumb and blind.

They are quick to observe and denounce the lack of justice [17] and brotherhood [18] in other countries around the world, but it's either too drunk, blind or guilty to notice and deal with any in its own.

You would think their churches would be tired by now of being pimped by the rich and powerful and condemned by the fatherless [19] and the poor.[20]

In the very same Bible in which they say their country is founded, the Prophets warned against these very same issues over and over again before the fall of their people.

But for all practical purposes, the American church is silent and impotent. The beloved American, Mark Twain, in 1900, wrote:

> "I bring you the stately matron named Christendom, returning bedraggled, besmirched, and dishonored from pirate raids in Kiao-Chou, Manchuria, South Africa, and the Philippines, with her soul full of meanness, her pockets full of boodle (money), and her mouth full of pious hypocrisies. Give her soap and towel, but hide the looking glass." *(Twain)*.

There are several other American writers who criticized America's Christianity also, if we can call it that.

And what about America's Democracy? Everyone knows it is no real democracy at all.

It's an oligarchy,[21] and it's always been one.

Their ex slave-holding president, George Washington, was the richest man in America during his time, and he was representative of all the founding fathers.

America's arrogance is unbelievable. She actually assumes she can grant her citizens the freedom that only God can give or take.

How dare she!

The American conquerors are no more ignorant now than the European conquerors were then, and in fact, they are even wiser.

Their plea of *innocence* [22] is insulting.

There have always been those voices crying out in the wilderness with the nerve and the wisdom to confront hypocrisy, lies and other evils. They just get ignored or slaughtered. Ask the Prophets. Ask the Abolitionists.

Even better, ask the New Abolitionists. [23]

Therefore, in consideration of all this reality, it would appear to be absolutely ludicrous for *any* right-thinking , real Christian in America *not* to question their allegiances, *wouldn't it?*

It would be as crazy as White Americans embracing the legacies of people like Nat Turner, John Brown, David Walker, and the Black Muslims.

Where Do We Go From Here, Part 2

Nevertheless, in spite of all the aforementioned factors, a significant number of us Black people here in America continue to reconcile and embrace it's legacy and inheritance.

Some say it's because we're a forgiving people. *Maybe so.*

I'm convinced, however, that most of us do so simply because we've become just as greedy and deceived as our ex-enslavers.

Just like the Jews in Babylon.

However, if indeed there are those of us who are that forgiving and capable of enduring all of this American racism and discrimination in order to establish the soul of this country, it would indeed be a Christian ideal.

This is referred to as redemptive suffering, and as hard as it is, it's what Christ did for all mankind and it's the highest form of nobility. [24] Along with passive resistance and moral agitation, it was the basis of Dr. King's non-violence movement.

However, I personally believe it would be nothing less than miraculous to see America show fruits worthy of repentance.

It would be as miraculous as seeing the proverbial camel make it through the needle"s eye, or more appropriately, the rich man selling everything and giving to the poor to follow Jesus.

Yet and still, just like Jonah knew it was possible for Nineveh to repent, I too know that it's *possible* for America to truly repent.

I just don't believe it's *probable*.

Therefore I'd propose three options for Black Americans as an answer to the question, "Where Do We Go From Here, Now?".

In spite of all the problems associated with being Black in America, I'm convinced most of us would like to stay here and carry on with business as usual. Just like the Jews in Babylon.

So that would be **Option One**. Those of us who chose to stay would either continue to suck the life out of this country from within its poverty cycle or strive to arrive at that wonderful and marvelous place that Dr. King dreamed of.

And if by the grace of God they were able to get America to truly repent, then and only then might this country be worth living in.

Option Two would be to separate from White Americans, yet remain in America. This could easily be accomplished by establishing a number of states as the primary habitation of Black Americans.

The number of states and the amount of federal representation should be proportionate to our population in this country. Other ethnicities that were willing to embrace us would be welcome as well.

In a Black America we'd manage the mainstream enterprises, markets and institutions within America's capitalist system. Consequently, employment and education discrimination would be far less significant obstacles to our welfare and advancement, along with several other benefits.

We would dominate the culture, and that doesn't mean we'd have a rap song for an anthem or soul food in the statehouse. What it means is we would have a more humane society and an environment where our children can escape the incredible odds of becoming yet another American victim.

And at the very least it would be a society where erasing racism would become a real priority, and that's a very important piece of what we need to arrest our disturbing trends and truly flourish.

I'm inclined to believe that, ultimately if not initially, this would be the most desirable lifestyle for the majority of Black people in America, *if we had the option.*

But for those of us who cannot continue to reconcile this country's legacy and heritage at all, we deserve the right to emigrate with adequate compensation and that would be **Option Three.**

Adios and sayonara ... simple as that.

Those of us who have already risen above our programmed fear and contempt for the Motherland, let alone the rest of the world, will quickly perceive this as a far greater option.

If we only knew why most White historians demonized Africa, why White conquerors wanted to own it, and why White colonists wanted to settle there, we'd be excited about going there too.

The unassimilated mind doesn't have to wonder why we had the hardest time getting them out of Africa in the first place or why the majority of tourists to Africa today are White.

Say what you will about Michael Jackson, but there are few greater advocates of our indigenous land and kindred than him. And he advocated from a position of one who's spent time and treasure on the continent, not a mediaholic.

Few Black folk seem to realize that Africa is still a very beautiful continent with beautiful people who are actually a lot more hospitable and less deceived than most Americans.

And little might we realize it but parts of Africa are no hotter than Arizona, New Mexico or "down south".

Years ago I wrote a poem that's applicable for the Black person who thinks about going home to Africa. It's called *"Songs of Zion"* and it's about the corruption of music, but it also says a little about the concept of "home".

As I mentioned earlier, the Jews were sent into Captivity in Babylon around about 600 BC, and after being released, very few of them chose to return home. [25]

Those who did were mostly the poor folks and the patriots, and it is this type of Jew who left us with the verses found in chapter 137 of the book of Psalms.

It establishes the basis for my poem.

> Scriptures still saturate
> Some of our brother's songs
> However here in this land
> You'll find them being strangled
> Asphyxiated and suffocated
> Have we forgotten Zion?
> From a cozy back-seat in Babylon
> It's easy to forget.
> While this mega-culture rushes
> Like a river to the new frontier
> Silent tears flow, from its soft, slow-kill
> All the way back home to Zion.
> Don't we remember home?
> From a cozy back-seat in Babylon
> It's easy to forget.
> The Holy Sounds have been sold out
> For a shady spot in paradise
> The captive's imaginations have been captured
> And the prisoner's motivations have been plundered.
> The songs of Zion have been seduced.
> And now no one remembers when
> Music was once serious business.

It's quite obvious that we Black folk here in America have forgotten home.

We might think we're "woke", but we're actually still thinking with our old colonized mind if we see under-class citizenship in this so called "Promised Land" as a blessing, and home as a curse.

We know that our authentic history and culture was corrupted and demonized by White educators, but we still have major difficulties conceiving that there could possibly be any positive aspects to home.

Few of us are aware that Black historians have proven that in general, African people and societies have always been characteristically peaceful, patient, religious, hospitable, practical, non-materialistic, improvisational, forgiving, just and ethical *(Paris)*.

As a result, our societies were able to last thousands of years prior to outside influences.

Little do we arrogant Black people in America know it, but we have more to gain from Africa than we have to contribute to it.

Several other enlightened Black people have been just as convinced of this and consequently returned there themselves or promoted the return of Black people to Africa.

Two of the better-known advocates have included Marcus Garvey and W.E.B. Du Bois, who's also known as the "father of the Pan-African (back to Africa) Movement".

But God forbid we repeat the mistake many of our past Black missionaries made. Let us not attempt to return home to Africa arrogantly as ex-Americans, coming to help save and lead the poor, defenseless and oppressed Africans.

They're not all as backwards or oppressive as the Western controlled media would have us to believe. Nor are they all starving or at war.

And anyway, concerning the atrocities that are in fact committed over there, who are the Americans to judge them? According to the global perspective of the impartial Amnesty International, they are nothing less than hypocrites to do so.

The only difference between Africa's atrocities and America's is that this country's are more covert, subtle and rationalized, which makes them more palatable for American appetites. Check out Amnesty International's website for more insight on the matter.

And regarding the needs that do in fact exist upon the continent, just think ... if we selfish and greedy Black people here in this country were ever to *mimic other minorities* and establish viable markets for our kindred's services and resources, then perhaps we could bless each other as well.

Little do we know it, but if we were ever to receive the proper compensation to go back home to Africa or migrate anywhere else in this great big world, it would be a more than adequate option to receive as America's *"fruits worthy of repentance"*.

In any case, the unique and creative aspect of all these three different options taken together is that they also address the ever-imminent reparations issue. It's only a matter of time before it has to be dealt with.

The Japanese and the Indians have already received their reparations from this country. And America was instrumental in obtaining reparations for Jewish Holocaust victims from the Germans as well, so let no one convince you that we don't rightly deserve them also.

The danger for us however is that if the matter of Black reparations is not handled properly it could make our stay in this country even more miserable.

There also exists the danger of being hoodwinked and receiving our payback in ungodly forms, such as casino money, lotto money, cigarette and alcohol money, etc.

Now from a White Americans perspective, I can only speculate of course. But it would seem to me that divorcing themselves from those of us who do not embrace this country's legacy or rhetoric at all would be very desirable. It should be worth the money to be free of us. No reconciliation required or desired.

Secondly, it would seem to me that partnering with those of us who actually consider it to be a real blessing to be here and enthusiastically embrace this country's stated ideals, in spite of its conflicting behavior, would be just as desirable.

This type of Black person feels as though they've already received their inheritance by just being here and is consequently already reconciled with America or is in the process of reconciling. They are an asset to this country.

Finally, it would seem to me that allocating separate American states for those of us who continue to embrace this country's legacy and heritage, yet don't believe America will ever rise above it's racism, would be a very conservative price to pay for the barbaric crime that was committed against us.

America should jump at the chance to finally be relieved of such intense collective guilt and punishment for their sins and the sins of their fathers.

They cannot continue to enjoy the fruits of their father's plundering and pillaging without being complicit in the oppression and abuse that results.

They know they are accountable! Their religious leaders know they've compromised the principles in Nehemiah 1:6-7. Haven't they told their congregations?

They also know that our contribution to their present illegitimate wealth has been immeasurable.

It's time for America to lose the "Innocent Act" and start bearing "Fruits Worthy of Repentance" if it truly possesses any real honor and integrity.

The same man who they honor with their lips on the third Monday of every January said some other things besides, "I Have a Dream..."

He also said: "The ultimate measure of a man is not where he stands in moments of comfort and convenience, but where he stands at times of challenge and controversy."*(King)*

And in his speech entitled, "Where Do We Go From Here?" he said: *"America, you must be born again!"*

As far as we Black people here in America are concerned, I can't suggest strongly enough that we also pursue a rebirth.

And I propose we prepare for it by reexamining the Jews' example in this matter as well.

Not long after they had been released from captivity in Babylon and allowed to return home, two of their religious leaders stepped up and began to institute a national restoration program.

The books of Ezra and Nehemiah mention many of the pivotal principles that our own religious leaders must start making a priority of if they ever intend to initiate our rebirth.

They are as follows:

They demanded respect for God's Word.

They demanded respect for God's House.

They demanded integrity and godliness from their spiritual and secular leaders.

They demanded separation from and opposition to intimate secular relationships and associations.

They demanded repentance and confession for personal and corporate sin.

They demanded the sanctity of marriages and families.

They demanded respect for their communities.

They demanded respect for their spiritual heritage.

They demanded unity.

They demanded the welfare of the poor.

They fervently opposed corrupt and oppressive power.

They fervently opposed greed.

And even though these men received their share of opposition, temptation and ridicule from the people living among them, they still dared to enforce these demands. Undoubtedly it was because they had experienced the consequences of compromising them previously.

For me personally, it's not really all that important whether we return to Africa or not. It's not really all that important whether we receive reparations from this country or our own separate states or not, although we do deserve them.

What's really crucial for me is that we all ultimately come to the same awareness that Ezra and Nehemiah came to.

And that is, the key to our future successes lie not in our own intelligence, power or luck. Nor does it lie in our oppressors fear or compassion. It lies in nothing less than our trust and obedience to:

The tried and true
The living and powerful
The reviving and liberating
The comforting, cleansing and convicting
The infallible, impartial and enduring
The satisfying and sufficient
The illuminating and inspiring
The dependable and incorruptible

Word of God.

So then, I conclude this commentary by asking a very crucial question for us again: Just where do we go from here?

It should be rather obvious by now, *shouldn't it?*

Let Us Go Back To God.

Amen

Quotes And Citations

Amazon.Com. "A People's History of the United States." Review. <http://www.amazon.com/>

Boesak, Dr. Allan Aubrey. "Farewell to Innocence." New York: Orbis Books, 1977

Brooke, John L. "The Refiner's Fire: The Making of Mormon Cosmology, 1644-1844." Cambridge: Cambridge University Press, 1996

Dillard, William LaRue. "Biblical Ancestry Voyage." Monrovia: Ra La- Ven Rue Foundation, 1989

Holy Bible: Contemporary English Version. New York: American Bible Society. 1995

Holy Bible: Easy to Read Version. Texas: World Bible Translation Center. 2001

Holy Bible: The New King James Version. Nashville: Thomas Nelson, 1982.

Hughes, Langston. "Harlem." Montage of a Dream Deferred. New York: Holt, 1951

Ignatiev, Noel, and John Garvey. "Race Traitors." New York: Routledge, 1996

King, Dr. Martin Luther. "Stride Towards Freedom." New York: Harper & Row, 1958

Laugh Yourself to Life. Dir. Spruce McRee. Perf. Jonathan

Slocumb, Videocassette. Warner Alliance Home Video, 1997

Loewen, James W. "Lies My Teacher Told Me: Everything Your American History Textbook Got Wrong." New York: Touchstone, 1995

Lotz, Anne Graham. Interview. The Early Show. Host: Jane Clayson. CBS. 13 Sept. 2001

Mc Dowell, Josh, "Evidence That Demands a Verdict." Nashville: Thomas Nelson Publishers, 1999

Meeropol, Abel a.k.a Lewis Allen: "Strange Fruit." Perf. Billie Holiday. Commodore Records, 1939

O'Neil, Dr. Dennis, "Human Biological Adaptability." California: Behavioral Sciences Dept, Palomar College, 1998-2005, <http://anthro.palomar.edu/adapt/>

Paris, Peter J. "The Spirituality of African Peoples." Minneapolis: Augsburg Fortress, 1995

Scott-Heron, Gil, "The Revolution Will Not Be Televised." Flying Dutchman, 1974

Sider, Ronald. "Rich Christians in an Age of Hunger: A Biblical Study." Illinois: Inter- Varsity Press, 1977

Sutton, William Josiah. "The New Age Movement and the Illuminati 666." Dayton: The Institute of Religious Knowledge, 1983.

Thomas, Janet. "The Battle in Seattle." Colorado: Fulcrum Publishing, 2000

Twain, Mark. "A Greeting from the 19th Century to the 20th Century". Commentary, New York Herald 30 Dec. 1900.

Whitfield, Norman J., and Barrett Strong: "Ball of Confusion." Perf. The Temptations. Gordy, 1970

Wikipedia. "Agape Feast." Florida: Wikimedia Foundation, 2001

Wilmore, Gayraud. "Black Religion and Black Radicalism." New York: Orbis Books, 1996

Wright, Pastor Joe. "The Prayer of Repentance." Kansas House of Representatives, Topeka. 23 Jan. 1996

Footnotes

---

[1]

    One of few German theologians who opposed Nazism.

[2]   Here's yet another example of American cultural duality; an intentional and purposeful mixing of evil elements among the good, or a mixing of the unnecessary with the necessary

[3]Early Black ministers knew this and drew parallels between their conditions and the Israelites in their sermons and writings. See Psalm 137.

[4]   My Bible says you're not qualified to be called a Christian if you habitually mistreat your neighbors.

[5]   The word "traps" or "snares" appear in most Bible versions an average of about 50 times. The word "net" appears about another 30 times.

[6]   From the poetry of Tupac Shakur.

[7]   The roots of racism can be found in this piece of garbage.

[8]*No one in their right mind would choose to be a prophet! See Luke 4:24 / Acts 7:52*

[9]Google the phrase "wealth gap in America"

[10]

    Few people remember Billy Graham's support of the Vietnam War and rejection of Civil Rights.

[11]   Janet Thomas, author of *"The Battle in Seattle"* summarizes the strategy used to fleece the Third World (pgs. 50-51)

[12]   Another good source for the other side of American history is a book by James W. Loewen, called 'Lies My Teacher Told Me: Everything Your American History Textbook Got Wrong".

[13]   The story behind this song is a must read.

[14]   John Maynard Keynes. His most popular expression was, "In the long run, we are all dead."

[15]   The Bible mentions deceit in some form about 150 times.

[16]   Oppress appears in some form more than 100 times in the Bible (op-

pressing, oppressed, oppressor, etc.)

[17]   The word justice appears over 100 times in the New KJV.

[18]   There are over 100 references to the proper treatment of 'strangers' in Scripture.

[19]   The word fatherless appears almost 50 times in the Bible.

[20]   The word poor appears almost 200 times in the Bible.

[21]   Rule of the rich.

[22]   As defined by Dr. Allan Aubrey Boesak, in "Farewell to Innocence".

[23]   Abolitionism has been resurrected by two young White Americans through the founding of "Race Traitors", an extremely radical Journal and Website well worth being aware of.

[24]   See John 15:13

[25]   1 Samuel 16: 14-23 / 1 Chronicles 15;16-24

www.ingramcontent.com/pod-product-compliance
Lightning Source LLC
Chambersburg PA
CBHW031356250726
48655CB00013B/2311